More Than Just a Number

More Than Just a Number

Julie Cannon

More Than Just a Number

© Julie Cannon 2024

All Rights Reserved

Cover Design by Cara Leverette

ISBN 978-1-955295-31-4

Unless otherwise noted, all Scripture quotations are taken from the Holy Bible, New International Version®, NIV®. Copyright © 1973, 1978, 1984, 2011 by Biblica, Inc.™ Used by permission of Zondervan. All rights reserved worldwide. www.zondervan.com. The "NIV" and "New International Version" are trademarks registered in the United States Patent and Trademark Office by Biblica, Inc.™

Scripture taken from the ESV® Bible (The Holy Bible, English Standard Version®), copyright © 2001 by Crossway Bibles, a publishing ministry of Good News Publishers. Used by permission. All rights reserved.

Scripture taken from the New King James Version®. Copyright © 1982 by Thomas Nelson. Used by permission. All rights reserved.

100 Manly Street

Greenville, SC 29601

CourierPublishing.com

PUBLISHED IN THE UNITED STATES OF AMERICA

ENDORSEMENTS FOR *MORE THAN JUST A NUMBER*

Julie is one of the most genuine people I know, which shines through in her writing. This book offers a new and inviting way to approach everyday life, focusing on what God values instead of the world. Using personal stories, Scripture, and biblical insight, Julie unpacks the Truth that can lead to freedom for every woman through Christ.

Melanie Ratcliffe
Director of Relational Evangelism
South Carolina Baptist Convention

This devotional is a must-read for every woman who has ever struggled with being defined by a number. We have a God who wants us to be secure in how *He* defines us as His precious daughters. We are more than a number on a scale or a report card. As His children, we are chosen, redeemed, loved, and precious in His sight. In this devotional, Julie gives biblical and practical insight on how to live in light of how Jesus defines you. She speaks out of her own battles with numbers and how God has given her freedom over that which the enemy would try to steal, kill, and destroy. You can experience the freedom Julie has experienced by leaning into the truth proclaimed in this devotional! It is a treasure I will use in my ministry to women for many, many years.

Eden Richardson
Women's Ministry Director
First Baptist Church, Rock Hill, SC

It has been delightful for me to watch how God uses Julie to bless others. She has a unique gift of encouragement. In these pages, you, too, will be blessed, encouraged, and inspired by the wisdom and love God has given her for people just like you!

Richard Blackaby
Experiencing God, The Ways of God

More Than Just a Number is an easy-to-follow road map to freedom for women who desire to *thrive* versus solely survive. I felt like I was having coffee or a coaching session with Julie as I was reading through this devotional Bible study. In classic Julie Cannon style, she is pointing us to the Word, to God, via the Holy Spirit — which is the only truth that can truly set us free of whatever "numbers" have distracted us from God's best version of ourselves and our lives, and, thus, our legacy. Thank you, Julie, for being obedient. Your transparency, your analogies, and your wisdom are refreshing! This will be a resource I use personally, and with others, to inspire, encourage and equip toward freedom anchored in their identity in Christ.

Dawn Otten-Sweeney
Certified Blackaby Ministries Coach, WDT LLC
(Women Determined to Thrive ministries and coaching);
Independent National Sales Director, Mary Kay

I had the incredible privilege of calling Julie my friend and pastor's wife. Our whole community adored her because she brought everyone into her life, her friends' list and her ministry. As I read this book, I realized that she has been able to do that very thing through the written word. Her stories allow you to step inside to see the relationship that she has come to know with Jesus. My prayer for you as a reader is that you will long to know Him in the very same way.

Ruth McWhite
Former Director of Women's Ministries, North Greenville University
Staff Counselor, Rocky Creek Baptist Church, Greenville, SC

As a woman who thrives on resources focused on everyday living while strengthening my Christian walk, this devotional definitely satisfied my need. Living in a society driven — and sometimes burdened — by numbers, Julie has selected focus areas that are so relatable and will help you rely on God's Word for deliverance. Well done! I highly recommend this devotional as a personal study or for a small group.

Kelley Cornish
Pastor's Wife and Women's Ministry Leader
Second Baptist Church, Aiken, SC

I am so grateful to God that He put it on Julie Cannon's heart to write this devotional. She speaks straight to the heart of the matter so many women struggle with in their day-to-day walk with the Lord. Julie's heart for the Lord shines through her stories and personal transparency. I believe God will use this devotional to help women grow in their spiritual journey by taking Julie's life experiences and insights and coupling them with Scripture to transform lives.

Angela Carter James
Education and Women's Minister
Brushy Creek Baptist Church, Taylors, SC

Julie Cannon beautifully captures the spirit of the Word of God in our daily lives and removes our focus from the numbers we think define us. In a culture where truth is hidden and reality is blurry, Julie helps Christians understand clearly how God pursues us and how we should pursue Him.

Shana Sands
Women's Ministry Leader
Kingdom Life Church, Greenville, SC

Julie does a wonderful job of creating a devotional that is both biblical and practical. She shares her personal stories and experiences, which women of any age can relate to. This study is encouraging, inspiring and applicable to real life. It teaches us that we are more than a number to God. I look forward to using this Bible study in a small group with other women.

Donna Coker
Women's Ministry Leader
Central Baptist Church, Darlington, SC

Dedication

To Stephen Cannon, my husband and my greatest champion: Thank you for your unwavering support with this project! Thank you for constantly inspiring and encouraging me to take the next step with the Lord.

To Natalie, Tyler, and Ruthie Cannon, my precious children: Thank you for always believing in "Mom" and for cheering me on every step of the way! I love you dearly.

Table of Contents

Introduction xiii
Week One: Limitless 3
    Hormone Havoc 5
    The Dreaded Scale 11
    Suiting Up 15
    Soup Only, Please 19
    Sneaky Squirrels: Securing Your Supply 23
Week Two: Fully Surrendered 27
    Scarlet Labels 29
    Six Water Pots 33
    Cover-Up 39
    On the Sidelines 45
    Filled to the Brim 51
Week Three: Dwelling Well 57
    A New Direction 59
    Faith at the Fountain 65
    Thirty-Seven Is a Good Age 69
    Two Months at Best 77
    Drinking the Cup 81
Week Four: Simplified and Sure 87
    Fleeing or Following: A Thousand Times No 91
    When Christ Calls Your Name 97
    On the Ninth Day of Christmas 103
    Multitudes: Most or Mostest? 109
    Rags to Riches 115
    Closing Comments: Withering Roots 121

Introduction

We live in a world defined by numbers. They are everywhere we go and define much of society. From the number on a scale to the number on a report card to the number of points on a scoreboard to the number of friends that liked a recent social media post to the number of dollars in a bank account to the number of direct reports to the number of years on the planet to the number of years single or married — the list is endless.

As we begin this Bible study, I want to ask, "Are you allowing a number to define you?"

People constantly try to portray success in numbers. Businesses report gains and losses, while churches count offerings and enrollment. I grew up as a preacher's kid and often heard the church approach to numbers called the "nickels-and-noses" mentality. Often, we allow our worst day to become the definition of who we are: the day the divorce was finalized, the day cancer was diagnosed, the day the dreaded birthday arrived, or the day the scale's reflection didn't meet our expectations. A number can help us meet a goal and be a healthy objective or leave us empty and depleted. We are all trying to reach the next number on our list.

Perhaps the most important question is if we are looking and trusting in the numbers that are important to God.

In my life, the pursuit of numbers has been an ongoing battle. The number I have often allowed to define me has been reflected on the scale. My struggle began as a freshman in college. In the fall of 1994, I arrived on the beautiful college campus of Furman University. From the age of seven, it was where I wanted to attend. Our family did not have the finances to send me there, yet God provided them. As a child of a minister and a stay-at-home mom, I was rich in spiritual heritage, yet not in material possessions.

I found myself on a campus with a lot of people who, in my opinion, were a lot skinnier, prettier, and wealthier than me. So, my striving for perfectionism began. I struggled with ascertaining that perfect image that does not exist. I started obsessively counting calories and working out in a frenzy so that the number on the scale would go down. If I allow it, even today, the number reflected on the scale is the one Satan will use to steal my joy.

The drive to attain the perfect number also drove me to find comfort in majoring in health and exercise science. I enjoyed this major and sought solace in helping others on their journey. During this time, I taught aerobics, worked in cardiac rehabilitation, and found my place helping others through personal training. But recently, the number that haunts me is the number of days I am here without my mom and dad. My mom died in 2012, followed by my dad in 2014. With each passing year, that number gets larger and the loss greater.

Throughout this book, I will share many raw experiences, and I hope these experiences will help you. Whether you are a teenager looking to find your identity or a post-partum mom dealing with hormone havoc, you will be reminded that your core is found in Christ. I pray you will allow God to work in your heart and life. I pray that you will see yourself anew as loved, chosen, accepted, redeemed, gifted, and appreciated. And I pray that the number you most readily identify with will cease to rule and reign over your thoughts, attitudes, and actions.

The theme verses for this study are Isaiah 43:18–19: "Forget the former things; do not dwell on the past. See I am doing a new thing! Now it springs up; do you not perceive it? I am making a way in the desert and streams in the wasteland."

So, grab your Bible and get ready to start this journey. And as you begin, hear your heavenly Father say loudly and clearly, "You are more than just a number!"

More Than Just a Number

Week One
Limitless — ∞

The overarching purpose of this book is to provide a pathway of freedom over the numbers that so easily define us. I in no way pretend to be an expert on the subject. Instead, I am still on this journey and simply offer a proposal that has helped me in my weakest moments and hope it might help you find victory as well.

As I have wrestled with my struggle with identity-defining numbers, I have continued to ask the following questions: What numbers matter to God? Could God's numbers offer help and victory over my number? What if the solution was in the form of the problem?

The first number I would like to propose matters to God and is the first step on the pathway to freedom. Do you remember the symbol for infinity from math class? It is the number that best describes the power of our incredible God. His power is unending. His knowledge is unending. His presence is unending. His love is unending. His forgiveness is unending. His mercy and grace are unending.

Revelation 1:8 proclaims, "'I am the Alpha and the Omega,' says the Lord God, 'who is and who was and who is to come, the Almighty.'" Jesus reminds us in Matthew 19:26, "With God all things are possible." Perhaps my favorite is from the apostle Paul in Ephesians 3:20 as he tries to capture the power of God: "Now to him who is able to do immeasurably more than all we ask or imagine, according to his power that is at work within us."

The initial step toward victory over pesky identity-defining numbers is to look at the only One with authority to define us and recognize that His is a number that knows no bounds or limits.

Let's take this first step toward freedom together this week as we focus on the uncreated One.

Pathway to Freedom
∞ + 0 + 1 = MTJAN

Day One
Hormone Havoc

When I turned the big forty in September 2016, I was a mess. It seemed my hormones had taken up a life of their own and, depending on which week of the month it was, would rule the roost. My husband started tracking the symptoms on a spreadsheet on his phone. He referred to it as different seasons — fall, winter, spring, and summer. It became something we would laugh about, assuming I was in the correct season to find it funny.

Spring was characterized by a happy and upbeat attitude, and summer was pretty level. A storm started to brew in the fall, and then winter hit. Winter was full of defeated thoughts and unstable feelings. I allowed my fluctuating hormones to dictate my world.

Now, I was good at hiding it. I used the masking skills I had developed as a preacher's child and pastor's wife. I felt as if my body could betray me. When I was diagnosed with an ovarian cyst that wreaked havoc on my system, I at least felt better. The doctor told me I was experiencing some peri-menopausal symptoms that could last for years before the real menopause began. What? I didn't even know such a phenomenon existed. However, it was real, all right, and uncontrollable. One thing was certain: Satan was using this against me in a big way. The cyst caused me to retain fluid, sending the number on the scale up. I focused on all the wrong things.

During this season, when my feelings and focus were all over the map, the Lord directed me to Isaiah 42. Read Isaiah 42:4–20. There is such great encouragement in these verses.

First, God speaks to our feelings. Verse 4 says, "He will not falter or be discouraged till he establishes justice on earth. In his teaching the islands will put their hope."

God is not affected by our feelings, disappointments, or failures. We may feel we are unraveling, but God is always in control. No matter how many setbacks we may have, He "will not falter or be discouraged." He will not fail us. Feelings change, but God never does.

Verse 7 reminds us that our enemy loves to blind us with feelings of depression, fear, and doubt. He will use any vulnerable area to gain a foothold to keep us from succeeding in our journey to complete physical and spiritual health.

What are your vulnerable areas? What numbers do you tend to rely on for validation?

_____

_____

_____

As you pray today, ask God to keep your eyes from being blinded by the enemy's deception and lies.

Then, in verse 9, God addresses the issue of our focus. The Lord says, "See, the former things have taken place, and new things I declare; before they spring into being I announce them to you." This is a call by God not to allow Satan to keep us in the past. Cling to "and new things I declare." Put your hope for the future in Him today.

List below what spiritual and physical new things you want to experience on this journey with Christ.

Next, notice all the verbs listed in verse 13:
- March
- Stir Up
- Shout
- Raise
- Triumph

According to Webster's Dictionary, triumph means "a great victory or achievement." This is God's plan for our lives. He desires that we have compete victory over the areas where Satan holds us back. Only God can secure victory, but it does require our participation through focus.

We will close our time together today by studying verse 16: "I will lead the blind by ways they have not known; along unfamiliar paths I will guide them; I will turn darkness into light before them and make the rough places smooth. These are the things I will do; I will not forsake them."

God says He desires to do the following:
- Take off the blinders that Satan applies.
- Guide and lead our journey, even when it is unfamiliar.

- Take our defeated darkness and turn it into victory — darkness into light.
- Make the rough places smooth.

I want you to think about your physical vision for a moment. I have a contact lens prescription that is -5.00. That may not mean much if you do not wear glasses or contacts. Let's say that my vision is extremely blurry without either glasses or contracts. One morning as I frantically got ready for work, I mistakenly placed my husband's contacts in instead of mine. Stephen's prescription is -1.00. In a panic, I screamed, "I can't see. I can't see. I'm blind." My husband, who is the much calmer one, quickly realized what had happened. It is amazing that we can take something as small as a contact lens, place it over our eye, and have immediate transformation: 20/20 vision. Even more amazing is that we can have the smallest irritants on that contact lens, and our eye will immediately reject it. It cannot tolerate any outside substance on the lens.

Much of our spiritual life is like the need for a corrective lens. When we rely on God's resources and trust His provision, we only need a small amount to correct our spiritual vision. But when we attempt to accomplish life in our strength, we will repeatedly try to exhaustion as we struggle with a wayward child, an unsatisfying job, or a failing marriage. The list is endless. Satan will undermine in those places where he has the biggest impact for derailment.

Suggested Prayer

Lord, I'm so thankful that You never change, even though my feelings often do. Please make the small changes necessary in my life so that I might have clear spiritual vision and focus on what matters in Your sight.

Day Two
The Dreaded Scale

I have always detested a scale. It sits in the bathroom or bedroom and looms in the background. It has a hidden agenda — one that affects my mood for the day.

When Stephen and I married, we received several shiny new scales at wedding showers. I remembered opening them and thinking, "Oh, a scale. I am so excited." I took them all back.

During college, I realized it was best if I did not weigh on them. When I did weigh, the reflected number dictated my outlook for the day. If it were a number I deemed acceptable, I would be upbeat and happy. However, if the number did not meet my approval, I was discouraged for days. I could not deal with the reality the dreaded scale presented. That number became my focus for a period. It would be all I could see when I sat down to eat, went to the grocery store, or took a walk. That number started to define me, which I realize now was such a sad reality.

This battle against the scale has affected me throughout the years. Now, we have one scale in the house. However, my husband is the only one who uses it. He will put it out, weigh, and squirrel it away so that I do not become entranced by the powers it seems to hold on me.

My hatred for the scale escalated when my youngest daughter, Ruthie, was five months old. I was struggling. It seemed there was always something to claim my attention. Laundry. Bottles. Diapers. Lunches to make. Homework to check. Our family was in overdrive, and I was stressed and overwhelmed. In those moments, I wondered who created the theory behind the six to twelve-week maternity leave. That is not nearly enough time to recuperate from bringing new life into the world.

At this point, we had a nine-year-old, five-year-old, and five-month-old. I was not feeling well and ended up with a bladder infection and at the doctor's office. As is usual with any doctor's visit, the nurse asked me to step on the scale. I obligingly obeyed — after stripping to the bare necessities. I took off my coat, bracelets, and shoes and laid my pocketbook and thermos full of coffee on the table near the scale. The nurse looked at me with a resigned look as though I might be a little unstable. Every ounce mattered in this battle.

I held my breath, and the number registered. I remember wondering how the number I saw was possible. I still weighed what I did when I went back for my six-week post-partum checkup. This was after weeks and months of working out and restricting calories. I was mortified and defeated. I smiled at the nurse and walked to the examining room. She had no clue about the internal battle waging or the spiritual warfare. I told no one, not even the doctor when he arrived to write my prescriptions for my infection.

While I waited on the doctor, I texted my husband to proclaim the news. I sent it with a frowny face and a few exclamation points. Stephen has always been my biggest champion and wrote back some encouraging words. They didn't register in my mind. Satan was attacking me with words like loser, fat, and unworthy. I had to get this mindset under control but seemed to be failing miserably.

Then, God directed me to the passage for today: Ephesians 4:17–24. Read these verses. We will study these verses today and, in more detail, tomorrow.

"You were taught, with regard to your former way of life, to put off your old self, which is being corrupted by its deceitful desires; to be made new in the attitude of your minds; and to put on the new self, created to be like God in true righteousness and holiness" (Ephesians 4:22–24).

I want you to circle the word "new" and underline the phrase "created to be like God."

If you had to describe yourself in three words, what would they be? List them below.

_____, _____, and _____.

As you reflect on the words above, are they positive or negative? In my current job as a high school counselor, I see daily that students have a much easier time talking about their perceived weaknesses and downfalls than they do their strengths. We, as adults, aren't much better. I have often allowed Satan to "darken my understanding" for long periods. I, too, often sit in darkness while the Lord beckons me to walk toward the light. I easily focus on the number on the scale instead of the power of my heavenly Father to defeat the enemy.

God made and designed us. Only one of us exists on this planet. Think about that for a second. My husband jokes that several versions of me exist, depending on what time of month you encounter me. But even then, only one Julie Cannon lives, for which most are perpetually thankful.

What number can affect your entire attitude? As you finish the second day of this journey, I want to encourage you to remember that the Lord holds complete victory over that number.

Write a prayer below, thanking the Lord for how He made and designed you and claiming victory over the number that holds you captive.

_____
_____
_____
_____

Day Three
Suiting Up

When my son, Tyler, was three, he loved to dress up as his favorite superhero. His mood for the day dictated which character he wanted to portray. It would often change on an hourly basis. From Buzz Lightyear to Batman to Darth Vader, he would become a new person. His voice would change, along with his actions, to emulate that of the costume. In one instance, my husband and I had to convince him that just because he was wearing a Buzz Lightyear costume did not mean that he could fly. This was after his valiant attempt to take flight from our coffee table.

Major events are often marked by dressing for the occasion. Even in everyday life, what we wear often determines what we will do. A few examples might include the following:

Graduation — The graduate wears a full-length gown and a goofy cap. This dress marks the transition from high school or college.

Wedding — The bride wears a white gown. Her marital status is about to change forever. She walks down the aisle single but leaves as a wife.

Military — A person joins as a civilian but leaves a soldier. A specific uniform identifies them as Army, Navy, Marine, Air Force, or Coast Guard.

Athletes — Once an athlete steps onto a field or court, they represent the team they play for. Sometimes, the nicest person in the world suddenly becomes a maniac when they wear their uniform.

Baptism — My favorite outfit that signifies identity change is the baptismal robe. I love seeing those who have been baptized walk back into the service. As their hair drips water onto the carpet, I am reminded of God's goodness and grace.

We also do this every day. We take off our pajamas and put on our clothes for the day. Often, what we wear determines where we are going: gym, work, school, church. We have a choice for the day of what we will wear. In the same way, we have a choice daily about how we will spiritually suit up in our fight.

Read Ephesians 4:17–24 again. Today, we will focus on the two ways Paul says we can live our lives.

Option 1 (Ephesians 4:17–19)

A futile mind that is darkened in understanding leads to alienation from the life of Christ. It is characterized by ignorance and a hardened heart toward the message of Christ — one that is disobedient to the instructions of Christ.

Paul, however, is speaking about non-Christians, but some of it could also represent a defeated believer. Futile means incapable of producing any useful result. This line of thinking will completely get us off the track where God has placed us.

As you reflect on this past week, where, if anywhere, do you sense this line of thought?

_____

_____

_____

Option 2 (Ephesians 4:20–24): "But"
　　The opposite of the above is abiding in the life of Christ, being sensitive to Christ's message, and obeying Christ's commands.
- In this life, we are not depending on our strength but trusting in God's strength.
- We are not following our hearts but are sensitive and open to what God wants for our lives, families, and ministries.
- We hear the Word of God and then obey what He says.

　　God wants us to experience option two. He did not create us to live apart from Him. People tell us we can self-improve and self-help in all sorts of ways. Most religions, in fact, try to change what we do to affect our behavior.

　　Although we can change the things we do, only Jesus can change who we are. Once He changes who we are, that changes what we do. This must be accomplished by renewing our minds, which is referenced in verses 22 and 24. We must daily renew our minds by putting off the old and putting on the new. Paul says this is key. We must put off the old and apply the new.

　　Are you suited up in God's armor daily? Are you praying over matters and leaving them at the foot of the cross, or do you place them down only to pick them back up the next day? I have included a prayer in the appendix that has proven vital to me. It is a prayer I use each day to suit up with the full armor of God.

　　Today, pray and ask the Lord to give you victory over the number(s) that cause you the greatest trouble as you commit to renewing your mind by praying on the armor of God.

Day Four
Soup Only, Please

One of my absolute favorite vacations is going on a cruise. I love the ongoing activities, upbeat atmosphere, and endless food display. There is something about a free buffet that attracts folks of all ages. I always go with good intentions and leave feeling stuffed. Most of the time, when I am at a buffet, I can't decide what I want and get a little of everything.

On one of our family cruises, each night at dinner, we were seated beside a family of six: mom, dad, son, and three teenage daughters. Although dinner was the one meal that wasn't a buffet, a person could order anything he wanted — including one appetizer, soup or salad, entrée, and dessert.

Every evening, I heard the same order from this family's table, which intrigued me. Of all the available options, the mom said, "Soup only, please." Out of all the choices, she settled for soup and crackers. The waiter was stunned and would try his hardest to get her to make other options. She chose the bare minimum when the price had already been paid for the meal. I watched this family every night for five days, and it broke my heart when I looked at her teenage daughters. I have no doubt that a war was being waged in this mom's life that was affecting her family.

God nudged my heart one morning during that cruise and spoke, "How often are you like that in your spiritual life? You nibble on very little when I offer a bountiful supply. You settle for less when Jesus already paid for the best available."

- As you continue this study, ask, "Where are you surviving when God wants to

see you thriving?"
- Are you living on less when His unending supply is vast?
- Take an honest inventory of your life today as I did while writing this devotional. Are you surviving on soup and crackers when the King of Kings has prepared a feast for you and your family?

Read John 19:1–16. I want us to examine and study the words of Pilate today. He attempted to control the uncontrollable. Pilate longed to free Jesus (4, 6, 10). In verse 11, Jesus answered Pilate: "You would have no power over me if it were not given to you from above. Therefore, the one who handed me over to you is guilty of a greater sin."

Read the first part of verse 11 again. We have no power over many things in life. I thrive on structure and control, which has always been one of my weaknesses. Satan loves to squirm his way into our lives and transfix us on things outside our realm of control.

John 10:10 says, "The thief comes only to steal and kill and destroy; I have come that they may have life, and have it to the full." Circle that word abundantly. Webster's Dictionary defines abundant as "existing or available in large quantities; plentiful." The Lord wants so much more for our life than we could ever imagine. I have often wondered how sad it must make Him when we live in survival mode.

Pilate was confused as to why the crowd would not release Jesus. He even referred to Jesus as a king and asked, "Shall I crucify your King?" (John 19:15). Oh, but he didn't realize Jesus was being crucified for the folks to whom he asked the question. Imagine yourself in that crowd. Jesus was crucified for you and me so that we could have abundant life. A life of abundance is characterized by joy, fulfillment, love, and fruitfulness.

Answer the following questions in the space below:
- If you had to give yourself a letter grade on each of the above words, how would you score?
- When you think about the last word, fruitfulness, where do you find yourself making the most impact on God's kingdom?
- Are you multiplying yourself by investing in others, or are you standing still?

_____
_____
_____

For a moment, think about treading water. I am not a strong swimmer. Okay, that's an exaggeration. I am a terrible swimmer. I am so bad, in fact, I made myself take swimming lessons when I was in college. One of the hardest things for me to do was to tread water for minutes at a time. I didn't like staying in one place. One day, I asked the teacher, "What is the point of this? I am working so hard and literally going nowhere." He laughed and said, "Just keep doing it." He was not very empathetic.

God reminded me of treading water as I wrote this devotion. Was treading a picture of my spiritual life? No progress. No forward momentum. No growth. Was I spiritually treading water? Was I surviving on soup when the buffet was around the corner? How about you?

The Lord who went to the cross for us does not want us to live a life of mediocrity. Pray and ask God to give you victory and progress in your spiritual life. You don't want to settle for soup and crackers when Christ has paid for so much better. Ask God to help you thrive spiritually, not simply survive.

Day Five
Sneaky Squirrels: Securing Your Supply

Since 2020, many words have become mainstream in our daily vocabulary that were rarely thought of before. Words and phrases such as social distancing, variant, isolation, and community spread seem to have become engrained into our daily speech.

In our house, quarantine quickly became the most dreaded word. It ascended to the top of the charts above phrases such as clean your room, no more electronics, and eat your vegetables. The word quarantine denotes isolation, restricted movement, and separation. The number of minutes spent in the house seemed to multiply.

In our home, the word has also been accompanied by other words such as anxiety, fear, and discouragement. Fear of being called over the intercom. Fear of being sent home. Fear of missing out on all the scheduled events. For my second grader, this is the third year interrupted due to COVID-19. God convicted me that the key is not the interruption but the attitude with which the interruption is met.

As I pondered these thoughts, I found myself in a familiar spot. One of my favorite things to do in the morning is sit on the porch and watch birds come to the feeder. When the weather is nice, this is my preferred place for my morning quiet time with my open Bible and a large cup of coffee.

Something that often appears when I am not paying close attention is a sneaky squirrel. These bird food thieves will climb to the top of the tree, jump onto the feeder, and claim some of the food for their own. As the bird feeder sways, the entire contents fall to the ground below. A full bird feeder is now left empty. I have discovered that squirrels have absolutely no fear whatsoever of my voice. They continue to lunge as if I can't see them and will only scramble to leave when I get within a short distance. I've also noticed that those sneaky squirrels are awfully persistent. They will leave, but as soon as they think I am not watching, they will reappear repeatedly and do the same thing.

As I watched this scene one morning, the Lord impressed upon my heart that sometimes our spiritual life can fall victim to a similar scenario. Our enemy often sends sneaky squirrels in the form of distractors that sneak up on us and leave us feeling empty, restricted, and depleted. They strike close to home and return repeatedly at vulnerable moments.

During a season characterized by much change, I wanted things to return to normal. As each event was removed from my calendar, I felt as though I was becoming a little more defeated and depleted. Our three kids were all struggling and wrestling with this, each in their own way. At times, I was not even sure how to help them. I am so thankful I know the one in complete control of everything.

God directed me to John Chapter 10. Take a moment and read John 10:1–10, 22–30. Four helpful things the Lord showed me from this passage follow:

Satan	The Lord
Seeks to destroy	Wants us to shelter in His strength
Provides noisy distraction	Speaks when we are silent and still
Squanders resources	Secures your future
Stays for a short time, inflicting damage where he can	Stays eternally. Hope in Him is long-lasting and forever.

Amidst the fear, anxiety, and stress, doesn't it seem so easy to let Satan deplete our spiritual supply of joy, peace, and hope? Often, we are the ones who place restrictions on what God can accomplish through our lives.

Jesus speaks bold assurances in this passage that we can stake claim to. In verse 1, He says, "Anyone who does not enter the sheep pen by the gate, but climbs in by some other way, is a thief and a robber."

A thief and a robber take something that is already in our possession. As you determine to take the next step in your number to the Lord, where do you sense Satan is trying to steal your peace, hope, and joy?

_____

_____

_____

_____

Each time the squirrel squanders my bird food, I must refill the feeder for the birds to feast on again. It is an active choice not to leave that feeder empty — one I choose to make time and again. We must make this same choice daily to refill our spiritual supply with God's Word. We must strive to dwell with Him and rest in Him alone intentionally. Let's refuse to limit access to the One who has the power to transform our lives.

Close your time with the Lord today by reading and praying Isaiah 26:3–4. Take these two verses and turn them into a prayer like the following: "Lord, I pray that You keep me in perfect peace. Help me to keep my mind focused on You and not let Satan sneak in and rob my peace and joy. I have complete trust in You, Lord, and know I can trust in You forever, for You are my everlasting strength."

In God, our infinite supply is everlasting.

Spend some time in prayer and reflection. Answer the questions in the space below.

- Are you currently allowing the Lord free reign in your life?
- What distractions must be removed so that God can have complete and total access?

_____

_____

_____

_____

Week 2
Fully Surrendered — 0

Now that we have taken time to examine our God's unending and unlimited power on our journey to freedom, we take the next step on the pathway. In the first step, we look up. In the second, we look within. What we see when we look up is unlimited, but when we look within, we are immediately taken aback by the limits. If the first number that matters to God is infinity, the second number that matters to God is zero. The apostle John captures it best in John 15:5: "I am the vine; you are the branches. If you remain in me and I in you, you will bear much fruit; apart from me you can do nothing.

Did you catch it? Jesus says He is the vine, we are the branches, and God is the gardener. The purpose of our lives is to produce fruit, not chase a number that haunts us. We will produce spiritual fruit naturally by staying connected to the vine: Jesus Christ.

Often, pruning is necessary to bring forth the most and best fruit. But apart from Jesus, we can do zero. Nada. Zilch. For God to do what only He can do, we must be fully surrendered to allowing Him to work. Fully and surrendered are two powerful words.

As you start this week, revisit your connection to the vine. Are you completely abiding in Christ? The word abide is mentioned eleven times in John 15 and over forty in the Gospel of John. The command is not to produce fruit but to abide. If you are not making the progress you desire, look closer at the source of your strength. When we do not abide in Him, we will not make any progress or produce any fruit. This is one of the greatest struggles in my walk with the Lord — being instead of doing. I am a true

Martha at heart.

I am cheering you on and look forward to continuing this journey with you as you begin week two.

Pathway to Freedom
$\infty + 0 + 1 = $ MTJAN

Day One
Scarlet Labels

Labels are everywhere we look. They are on cereal boxes, ketchup bottles, and hair spray containers. A label directs us on what to do or not to do with the contents. There are designer labels, and then others seek to imitate the original.

Often, labels are placed on people as well. While people labels are not written, they are no less powerful. As a school counselor, I see it every day. The student who did not behave well in one grade becomes labeled as a discipline problem in the next. An adult who chooses to leave his spouse is referred to as the divorcee. A teenager living in sin is labeled as rebellious.

Labels are easily applied, based on both attitudes and actions. Aren't you thankful that God doesn't refer to us in terms of labels? The worrier, the doubter, the pot stirrer. God's labels are different. For example, whenever we ask, He applies His forgiven label. And God's labels take the form of incredible gifts such as chosen, accepted, redeemed, gifted, and saved. I'll take those labels any day. God can take the most unlikely person, peel back any label, and apply His in its place.

Today, we will study one lady with a less-than-desired label. She would have been met with eye rolls and disdain had she graced the doors of the average church. Yet, God used her powerfully. The label applied by her hometown did not stand a chance against the grace of God.

In the passage you read today, you will see how God often uses ordinary and unlikely people to do extraordinary things for His glory. Have you ever applied a label to someone? Has one ever been applied to you?

_____
_____
_____
_____

Some labels we are born with, but others we acquire over time. One often applied to me is preacher's kid, or P.K. for short. I must admit I never wanted to be referred to as that.

When I was eight years old, I remember getting one of the worst spankings of my life. My friend and I thought it would be fun to hide from my parents after a night of Vacation Bible School at the church where my dad pastored. In the end, we slipped away from our teacher and found a cozy hiding spot in the baptismal pool. We heard people calling our names, and as the minutes passed, I soon realized I would be in serious trouble. We panicked, but instead of coming out of hiding, she and I hid farther into the crevices of the church behind the baptistery. It was not my finest moment.

The thing about applying labels and hiding is that the more we do it, the easier it becomes. Spiritually speaking, the farther we slip into the shadows, the more the shadows become the norm.

Read Joshua Chapter 2. As you read this chapter, you will see two of God's premier prophets hiding out in the home of Rahab. Pray and ask God to show you if there is an area of your life where He needs to unveil the mask so that He can work more abundantly in your life.

As you read this chapter, are you not amazed at the strength of Rahab? She went to extraordinary lengths for her family. She could have chosen the easy path. She could have sent the spies away. She could have chosen to believe any one of those ugly labels spoken about her. Instead, she exemplified courage, determination, and some spunk when she hid the spies and diverted those searching for them. She actively chose to peel off the old label and apply a new one.

In today's society, we often see the wrong heroes being praised. Our children are taught from an early age through television and social media to worship heroes of the wrong type. From sports to entertainment, the focus is often placed on worshipping those who make a lot of money and are in the spotlight.

Rahab was a different kind of hero. She made a bold declaration to the spies. She knew the Lord was with them and had blessed Israel. She desired the same for herself and her family (verses 9–13). Rahab was tired of following what the world offered. She wanted more for her family.

Answer the following questions in the space provided:

- Would the Lord say the same about you? Is that a picture of your life today?
- Are you desiring God's plan and seeking His protection for your family, or are you relying on your own plans and completing them in your strength?

Satan is extremely deceptive; however, he is not very clever. If you think about where he attacks you most often, it is probably the same area. He will zone in on your weakness and continue to use it against you. He will attempt to defeat you with that number. Spend some time claiming God's victory over that area today. God has already won the battle, so extinguish those fiery darts in His power and strength rather than your own. The cord that saved Rahab and her family was scarlet (18, 21). The scarlet blood of Jesus that ran from the cross is sufficient for whatever is holding you back today.

Consider the following questions:

- Are you hiding out, spiritually speaking? Are you allowing Satan to hinder what God calls you to do because of fear or comfort?
- Is there a label that needs spiritual removal?
- Are you relying more on what the world offers than on God's abundance?
- Is God calling you to take a bold stand for the Lord at your job, school, athletic team, or family?

Drop the scarlet cord and allow God to do what only He can by demolishing the number that is holding you back today.

Day Two
Six Water Pots

It was Mother's Day. I looked at my youngest child and said, "Ruthie, you are my baby girl."

She looked at me and said, "I am not your baby. I am a big girl now. I am growing up."

Her comment made me sad. On this particular Mother's Day, my kids just looked older. Their numbers were definitely changing, and as a mom of a fifteen-, eleven-, and six-year-old, it was bittersweet. This was also the seventh Mother's Day since my mom had died. Mother's Day had become a day to remind me that my mother was gone, as if I needed a reminder. I told myself that morning that I would focus on the blessings of God and who was present in my life, instead of those who had gone on before me. Satan will make a valiant attempt daily to steal what God has given us.

That morning, my husband preached from John 2. I did not even want to go to church. I did, but tried to hide that morning. As a pastor's wife, I have a difficult time doing that. I sat on my pew and took notes. I could not sleep that night, and God directed me back to this passage. He clearly led me to focus on the six water pots. This is where I want you to focus today. Read John 2:1–11 and focus on verses 5–7.

Imagine six water pots large enough to contain twenty to thirty gallons each. Jesus' instructions in verse 7 were to fill the jars with water. They filled them to the brim. I can close my eyes and see the water sloshing over the edge. God spoke to me through this passage and said, "Julie, you need filling up like that water pot."

As you focus on these water pots, think about their characteristics and if these same words could describe your spiritual life.

Empty — We typically think of the word empty in a negative context. However, today I want you to think about it in the opposite way. The water pots were sitting by the wayside, waiting to be filled. Often, we get distracted by the world's opinion of what we should be filled with. From our status on social media to the amount of money we have or lack thereof in our bank account to the number on the scale, we can allow these thoughts to overcome us. God nudged my heart to realize this happens when we fill up on things other than Him.

Who or with what would you say you are filling up with today?

_____

_____

_____

My battle with the number on the scale has dominated my thoughts for many days. I have been so controlled and full of battling the image in my mind that I have not allowed God to rule and reign in my life. I have often heard the lies that I was not good enough, beautiful enough, tall enough, or skinny enough. My water pot was filled with negativity, doubt, and insecurity during those times. God wants to fill us to the brim with assurance, peace, comfort, and security. Will you allow Him to do that today?

Ready — Mary looks at the servants and says, "Do whatever he tells you" (5). I can only imagine what they were thinking. They were standing around waiting on the guests and serving the food and wine when this unknown man told them to take empty water pots and fill them with water. It sure seems this was a ridiculous solution for solving their wine crisis. However, if they doubted him, they didn't show it. No hesitation. They were ready.

Are you ready for God to show up in a mighty way in your life? Or are you stalled out and sitting on empty?

When I worked as a high school guidance counselor, I was across the street from my daughter's elementary school. I had to leave for her award's day program one winter day. My husband had told me if he had time, he would swing by and pick me up so we could ride together. I got in my car and turned it on when he pulled into the high school parking lot. I jumped out of the car and into his car, only to forget to do one thing. When I returned after Natalie's program, I found my car still running. It had idled for over an hour. It was such an old car that I was a little disappointed no one had taken it.

We must be ready to move when God says move and to go when He says go. Like that car running in place, we often must be turned on and ready to redirect when God shows us what our next assignment is.

Patient — Are you waiting on God's timing? Is there anything you are praying over right now that you are ready for God to hurry up and answer?

When Mary initially approached Jesus, He said, "Woman, why do you involve me?

... My hour has not yet come" (4). Basically, He is saying not yet. I am not sure what transpired between Jesus and his mom between verses 4 and 7, but in verse 7, He gives the instructions to fill up the water pots. It was time for Him to begin His public ministry.

Make this your prayer this week: "Lord, I am going to wait on Your timing, plan, instructions, and word before I make a move."

Available — How available are you when it comes to being used by God? Do you place parameters on how and where He can use you?

When God called my husband to a previous church ministry, God spoke to me one night as I prayed. It was an early October morning, and He said, "Julie, I will provide you with a job, yet it will not be in the way you expect." That was it. I remember asking for more details. I wanted further instructions.

It was not until the end of April that God showed me His will for me was to work part-time at an elementary school and part-time with the student ministry at the church. I could not have been more surprised. I went from high school students to elementary and from preschool ministry at our previous church to teenagers and college students.

Our attitude and availability will often determine our assignment. If we provide our availability, God will take care of supplying the ability.

Audience — I have often heard my husband say, "Say yes to Jesus, no matter what He asks. You must place your yes on the table before the question is posed." Mary was a teenager, completely devoted to God, when she was told she was with child. In this passage, she was the one who encouraged Jesus to get started with His public ministry.

As a mom, I can relate to the reality that we can get away with saying things to our children that others cannot. Mary was in Jesus' audience. She was His biggest fan — His encourager. Mary had unwavering faith in her son's abilities.

Who is in your audience? Who are you choosing to surround yourself with?

Great Faith — Verse 8 says, "Then he told them, 'Now draw some out and take it to the master of the banquet. They did so.'" I want to close by focusing on those last three words: They did so. Spend a moment thinking about what was on the line for these servants. If they had taken unsavory water or wine to the master of the banquet, they would have messed up. They were the only ones who knew what had happened.

My dad preached for thirty-two years. When we had an amazing church service, he always said, "The real preacher showed up today," meaning the Holy Spirit was at work in a way that only He could. On this day, the real Master showed up. He took six dusty, empty, worn-out water jars and performed His first miracle to kick off His public ministry. It's a beautiful picture — an empty vessel filled by the Master.

As you reflect on these statements, where are you struggling the most?

- Are you filling up with the wrong things? Do you need God to empty you of those distractors keeping you from drawing close to Him?
- Are you ready to go when God says go?
- Are you patient and abiding by God's timeline?

- Are you available to go whenever and wherever God calls?
- Who is in your audience? Whose audience are you in?
- Do you have great faith? Are you praying with expectancy?

Spend some time in prayer, asking God to fill you to the brim as only He can.

Day Three
Cover-Up

It was summer and finally time for our vacation. Since Christmas, we had been counting down the days, and the dry-erase board in my office now read zero. As we arrived at the beach, I knew I was facing a battle in my mind regarding the menacing swimsuit. The war was waging. I was hearing, "You still haven't lost those post-pregnancy pounds. Are you wearing that? You should wear a cover-up." Continual thoughts echoed in my mind.

By Wednesday of that week, I had had enough. I was miserable because I was allowing Satan to feed me a steady diet of lies. While there was truth to the fact that I had not lost weight, it was not true that I needed to be ashamed of my body. Flawed was what Satan wanted me to hear and feel.

I got up early the following day, and the Lord directed me to Isaiah 57:14–19. That is where we are going to camp out today. God nourished my soul with these words. Look at the following from this passage:

- "To revive the Spirit of the lowly."
- "I will guide them and restore comfort to Israel's mourners."
- "'Peace, peace to those far and near,' says the Lord, 'and I will heal them.'"

I needed mental and emotional reviving and healing from those attacks regarding my body image. The number for me that summer haunted me wherever I went. It stalked me at the grocery store, the beach, and the doctor's office. It wasn't until I claimed God's promises that I relinquished those doubts and thoughts. I continually trusted my strength to overcome these attacks, so they often sent me reeling. When I began to focus on the number reflecting at me from the scale, it affected my entire attitude.

The thought of a cover-up was a symptom of a larger problem I faced. It was the desire to hide. Your battle may be similar, or it could be a completely different number that Satan uses to taunt you. Whatever your number is, cling to the fact that God can provide you with healing and comfort. Wanting to fit into any other image than the one God created you to be is a lie from the master of deceit.

I made myself go shopping for a new bathing suit. As I entered that section of the store, I could see the looks on the women's faces. Many were scouring the section for the one suit that glorified their good spots and hid the less desirable ones. I had no idea how many versions of suits existed. The bathing suit bottoms all had names such as cheeky, boy short, and bikini. I even found a few labeled extra cheeky. The last one was definitely not for me. I laughed as I looked at the bathing suit names and the grimaces on women's faces. I finally just grabbed a few and headed to the dressing room. I left that day feeling defeated, thinking about the sizes I had chosen.

The Lord does not want us to camp out in the valley of defeat. No matter the number Satan attacks you with, you have a refuge in the Lord.

Read Psalm 46:1–5.

Webster's Dictionary defines refuge as "a condition of being safe or sheltered from pursuit, danger, or trouble." Where or in what are you seeking refuge as you work toward restoration? Record your thoughts below.

Cover-Up

God wants us to seek refuge in Him when we are overwhelmed or defeated. This has been a journey for me over the last twenty years. There have been seasons when I needed a refuge for a longer period than others.

I needed a refuge when my dad died two short years after my mom. We were changing churches, homes, and communities. My dad was under hospice care, and it was during December. December is typically a month for joy, but I was defeated. The number I wanted then was more days with my dad. I can remember sitting with him during one of his last days and telling him it would not be long until he saw Mom again. He smiled and said, "I will tell her all about Ruthie." At that time, Ruthie was eight months old. I kept it together until I broke down into a thousand shattered pieces in the hall.

God is all the following for us:
- Refuge
- Strength
- Very present help in trouble

Verse 5 says, "God is within her; she will not fall." God wants us to run to Him. He is the ultimate cover-up. He will cover us with mercy, grace, peace, and love. When Satan floods our minds with feelings of inadequacy, guilt, or grief, claim God's promises over them. God has already won the victory. It is ours today for the asking.

Many times, our expectations set us up for failure. In my case, I had the unrealistic expectation that I would quickly rebound to my pre-pregnancy weight at the age of thirty-seven. Our expectancy should be placed in the Lord, not ourselves or our ability to control the situation.

We have been covered with the precious blood of Jesus Christ. That is the only covering that we need. Spend some time today reflecting on God's goodness and grace. Think back to your salvation experience and write it in the space below.

_____
_____
_____
_____

If you are reading this and you do not know the Lord, take a moment and check out this acronym for the gospel or the good news found in Jesus Christ.

God created us to be with Him (Psalm 100:3).
Our sins separate us from God (Romans 3:23).
Sins cannot be removed by doing good things (Ephesians 2:8–9).
Paying the price, Jesus died for our sins (1 Corinthians 15:3–4).
Everyone who turns to Jesus alone will have eternal life (John 3:16).
Life that's eternal means being with God forever in heaven (John 17:3).

If you want to ask Jesus to save you from your sins so that you can live forever with God in heaven, then pray the following prayer:

Dear God,

I admit that I have sinned and need a Savior. I believe that Jesus came, that He died on a cross to pay the price for my sins, and that He rose from the dead to conquer death and sin. Right now, I confess Him as Lord of my life. I turn from my sin and myself and ask You, Jesus, to forgive my sin and save my soul. Amen.

If you made this decision today, please know I rejoice with you. Take a moment and let someone know about the decision you made.

Day Four
On the Sidelines

Our family loves sports. My oldest daughter Natalie plays tennis, my son Tyler is a basketball fanatic, and Ruthie claims volleyball as her sport. We live in a world dominated by the love of high school, collegiate, and professional sports.

As I prayed through today's devotion, God led me to Joshua 9–10. Read Joshua 9–10. God brought me to the following phrases: watching from the stands, waiting on the bench, or playing in the game.

Today as we begin our study, I want you to think about whether you prefer playing in the game, waiting on the bench, or watching from the stands. Record your answer with your explanation below:

_____
_____
_____
_____

I didn't know exactly what the phrases meant when God first impressed them on my heart. As I began to seek His will and pray harder, He showed me. Today's devotion stepped on my toes a little, so grab your closed-toe shoes and get ready to dig into some powerful Scripture.

The Gibeonites allowed fear to lead them to act deceptively in Joshua 9:24. They went to Joshua at Gilgal and asked for a treaty because of Joshua's reputation with the Lord. The leader's fame had spread throughout the land. They carried dry and crumbly bread with them to indicate the length of their journey (9–12). I am amazed by the length we sometimes go to carry out an act of deception. Only three days after this treaty was made, their deception was revealed. They went to great lengths to scheme and plan, but within days, their plot unraveled.

"The Israelites sampled their provisions but did not inquire of the Lord" (9:14). Those last seven words carry much weight. The Israelites started to rely on their wisdom instead of seeking God's will. Think about your current walk with the Lord.

- Does this characterize you? As you attempt to defeat your number, are you walking in your own strength or relying on and resting in God's strength?
- Are you allowing fear to rule, reign, and motivate your actions? Satan will use fear to debilitate and spiritually disarm you if allowed.

As you think about releasing the number's hold on you, envision a scoreboard. The number of points on the scoreboard always mattered to me in high school. I would watch my friends play football, volleyball, and basketball and cheer loudly for them to win. I played tennis, and my mood was invariably better when I walked off the court with a win versus a loss. It is difficult to watch a person or a team we love lose. Now that I am a parent, I think nothing is more complicated than watching our kids play. I want to actively give pointers that my oldest two children do not appreciate.

As I stated earlier, God placed specific phrases on my heart as I prepared this devotion. As you read over these three phrases, which one would you say describes your spiritual life? Take an honest inventory of your current condition. God can only work in our lives when we humble ourselves before Him.

Watching from the Stands
Think about this phrase and all it implies. Being a spectator in the stands means we came to view the action and will either applaud or grumble at the outcome. As soon as the game is over, we pack up and leave. We may root for a particular team but have no vested personal interest in the outcome. It always amazes me when someone in the stands talks about what we did when referring to a team — as if they lifted weights, trained, caught passes, or made baskets. Spiritually speaking, watching from the stands is characterized by the following:

- Lethargy
- Absence of a quiet time
- Deficient prayer life
- Sporadic church attendance. Or you may attend church yet not spend time on your own seeking God's will and direction.
- Disengaging in the spiritual fight for your children, marriage, and families.

Waiting on the Bench
One of my good friends coaches a high school girls' basketball team. She once told

me that one of her least favorite things to do is to sit players on the bench. She said the players would often move down the bench closer to where she was, attempting to get her attention. She said, "It is like they think I have temporarily forgotten they are on the team."

Waiting is difficult and requires stillness and patience. There will be seasons in our spiritual lives when God will have us be still and wait for His command. We must sit patiently while we listen for His voice to give our next instructions. Don't tie your self-worth to the amount of playing time you are given. Instead, be ready when your name is called to jump up and hurry onto the court for whatever is asked of you.

Playing in the Game

The following words and phrases immediately came to mind:
- Active
- Armed
- Engaged
- Ready for action
- All in. Whatever God calls you to do, you are willing to say yes.

Spend some time in prayer and ask God if there is an area in your life where you are allowing fear to prevent you from doing what God wants. Are you watching the stands, actively waiting on the bench, or playing in the game?

Close today by focusing on the following verse: "The LORD said to Joshua, 'Do not be afraid of them; I have given them into your hand; not one of them will be able to withstand you'" (Joshua 10:8).

    Notice that the verb give is in the past perfect tense. The action was already completed. The same is true today. God has already fought and won the battle you are waging.

Day Five
Filled to the Brim

I have never considered myself a prideful person. I never had a lot to be prideful of when it came to material possessions. I remember my college freshman year move-in day.

God had provided the tuition for me to attend. My dad was a minister, and my mom stayed at home. It was completely a blessing from God that I could go to a school that cost $35,000 annually.

I arrived on campus in an old Ford Taurus that had seen its better days. It was not impressive to those who had so much more. I struggled with inadequacies. I was constantly comparing myself to those around me, and through my distorted vision, I was falling short. My spiritual vision was blurred.

I remember my brother-in-law, Mark, helped me move in. After he installed our room's carpet, he pulled out his wallet and handed me a one-hundred-dollar bill. He said, "Use this any way that you see fit." It was an act of generosity that, many years later, I have never forgotten. Mark exuded a humble heart.

My dad was hospitalized during this time and couldn't help me move in. I can remember my mom and me eating lunch before she returned home. I stood on the sidewalk at Furman University and waved goodbye. Looking back, I realize my mom was facing an unbelievable spiritual attack with my dad in the hospital and her leaving her baby daughter at college. I never knew it. She hugged me, told me she would see me later, and drove off. As I reflect on this time in my life, I remember this moment with pride because of the internal strength my mom possessed.

But pride in the wrong moments of life can be costly. I was on a beautiful college campus, surrounded by people with a lot more in the way of material possessions — shinier cars and the latest and newest electronics. However, I would later find out that many were struggling with their own inadequacies.

Today, we are going to study John 16. Read John 16. Think about moments of pride in your life — the good and bad ones and then answer the following questions:
- When and where have you allowed pride to rule the roost?
- When have feelings of inadequacy stopped you from being all God wanted you to be?

_____
_____
_____
_____

I want you to imagine an overflowing cup as you begin today's study. One that is filled to the brim and sloshing over onto whatever is around it. That is exactly what I think we look like when the Holy Spirit leads our lives. This is evident when we walk into our workplaces on Monday morning, sit in the car line, or stand in line at the grocery store. We look different.

I am forever thankful for the working of the Holy Spirit. There have been many times when the Lord has spoken to me through the prompting of the Holy Spirit. It is never God's desire for us to be confused about His will for our lives. When we have a decision to render, a path to choose, or a choice to make, we can rest in the guiding knowledge of the Holy Spirit.

Before you dive into this passage, pray that God will speak to you through these verses. Ask Him to lead you to a verse you can cling to this week. He will be faithful to answer if you listen to His voice.

How did you sense God speaking to you through this passage?

_____
_____
_____
_____

I remember clear direction from the Holy Spirit when I was a sophomore at Furman University. The entire Baptist Student Union (BSU) studied Experiencing God that fall. This was at such a pivotal time in my life. I grew up going to church every time the doors were open. It was not a decision I had to make. It came with being the daughter of the pastor.

When I arrived at college, I was searching. I had to decide whether my beliefs were my own or a product of being the preacher's kid. God had provided my tuition, for which

I was grateful. However, I felt financially broke most days compared to those on campus. So, I worked several jobs while at Furman to compensate.

For fall break that year, my family and I went to the beach. One of my dad's good friends was pastoring a church in the area and had recently undergone heart surgery. One day as I was completing my Bible study, the Holy Spirit prompted me to give all that was currently in my checking account to this pastor and his wife. It was not a large sum, but it was all I had to last for the remainder of that semester. I remember wrestling with the Lord over this. A day passed, and I did not obey. On the second day, I gave the Lord a list of names who could give more than me. By the third day, I was miserable.

I remember telling my parents I had to run an errand. I went to Bobby and Grace's house with no idea of what to expect. As I sat in their living room, I explained what God had laid on my heart. I gave them the check and walked out the door. As I drove back, I prayed that God would supply my needs as He saw fit. The following day, Grace called to let me know the check was for the exact amount they needed to pay off a lingering hospital bill.

The following week, I returned to my on-campus job at the health and wellness center. I received a phone call from two students who wanted personal training for the balance of the semester. God not only resupplied that income, but He also tripled it. I wish I could write that I have always obeyed the Spirit. I am ashamed to say there have been times when I have avoided an uncomfortable conversation about salvation, not written a check He asked me to give, or walked across the street to invite a new neighbor to church. But on that day, I learned a valuable lesson about the prompting of the Holy

Spirit. When He speaks, the only answer is "yes." He will always provide when He calls us to complete a task.

John 16:23–24 says, "In that day, you will no longer ask me anything. Very truly I tell you, my Father will give you whatever you ask in my name. Until now you have not asked for anything in my name. Ask and you will receive, and your joy will be complete."

- Are you answering with a yes when God calls, or are you debating with Him?
- Is your will aligned with His?

Several years ago, my husband, Stephen, preached a sermon about the work of the Holy Spirit. I had the following notes in my Bible that I hope are as meaningful to you as they were to me. As you finish this week, give praise for the working of the Holy Spirit in your life. Look up and write these verses in the margin. Pick one or two to memorize this week.

7 Roles of the Holy Spirit
- Creation — Genesis 1:2
- Conviction — John 16:8
- Conversion — James 4:8; Acts 2:37–39
- Comfort — John 14:27
- Counsel — John 16:13
- Correction — John 14:26
- Change — John 14:12

As you look at this list, where have you experienced the Holy Spirit working in your life?

_____

_____

_____

_____

On one Wednesday night, a teenager came up to me after the service. She had tears streaming down her face and said, "I have never felt this before. Tonight, God spoke to me during the message, and I know He is calling me to missions. He also showed me I need to give up a bad habit I have formed."

We prayed together. She experienced conviction, correction, and change that night. There is nothing that people can manufacture that even slightly resembles the moving of the Holy Spirit. Once you have experienced it, it leaves you wanting more.

Pray that the Holy Spirit will work and move this month like He never has before in your life, marriage, family, and church. Pray that your cup will overflow with the joy only He can provide.

Week Three: Dwelling Well
Depend, Dwell, and Delight

I hope that by week three God is speaking to you. My prayer is that you have encountered Him in the sweetest and most personal way. This week you are going to focus on where and how you are spending your time. In other words, are you dwelling well? Time is incredibly precious. At the end of our days, the only number that will have mattered is how we chose to spend the time we were blessed with.

So far in our journey toward becoming more than just a number, we've seen that the first number that is important to God is that of infinity. His power is limitless. The second number that matters to God is 0. It means that we recognize what we bring to the table — ZERO! The final number that matters to God is 1. Simply put, we gain victory over the numbers that define us ONE day at a time. In Luke 9:23, Jesus says, "Whoever wants to be my disciple must deny themselves and take up their cross DAILY and follow me."

Finding victory requires that we look up to a God whose power is infinite, look within as a reminder of our shortcomings, and then do so every day, one day at a time. If you are like me, you probably are good at giving things over to the Lord to control, only to pick them up in your own strength again. When we do this, we quickly snatch defeat from the jaws of victory.

Pathway to Freedom
$\infty + 0 + 1 = MTJAN$

Day One
A New Direction

As you begin today, answer the following questions in the space provided:
- Would you consider yourself good at following directions? From your boss, coach, spouse, co-workers, parents, or grandparents?
- Are you easily led? Are you more compliant or more argumentative when given a task to complete?
- In the past, when God has given you a new assignment, how willing have you been to accept it?

_____
_____
_____
_____
_____

I have never been good at following directions, especially in the kitchen. One of the reasons I often fail at a recipe is that I start to improvise about halfway through. When Stephen and I were newlyweds, I cooked multiple times a week. I tried to cook as healthy as possible. One recipe suggested replacing a cup of mayonnaise with a cup of plain yogurt. Plain was the optimal word. In my hurry at the grocery store, I had grabbed strawberry yogurt. That chicken divan casserole had a slightly "different" taste to it.

Directions are only good if followed. That is a statement I often heard in the halls of the elementary school where I worked.

In the passage today, we will examine the life of Joshua. Read Joshua 1:1–5.

The first five words in Joshua 1:1 are so powerful: "After the death of Moses … ." Don't skip those words because they carry a lot of weight. This was a pivotal time in the life of the Israelites and certainly in the life of Joshua. Their beloved leader, Moses, had died. However, it was not time to sit down and quit. God had a new leader in place to follow his original instructions (3). Although the leader had changed, God's plans had not (5).

Joshua was given new instructions and a new assignment. The Lord gets right to the point when He says, "Moses my servant is dead. Now then, you and all these people get ready to cross the Jordan River into the land I am about to give to them — to the Israelites. I will give you every place where you set your foot, as I promised Moses" (2–3).

As I think about the times when the Lord has given me a new assignment, I have always had a lot of follow-up questions for Him, predominately a lot of what-if questions. Often, I go into the plan thinking about a plan B. It is good to plan, but we should never get into the business of back-up plans. God's plans are always best and fail-proof.

What was the last assignment God gave you? It could have been an individual plan or one for your family to follow. How faithful were you in completing what He called you to do?

A New Direction

As I write this devotion on an early Saturday morning, God is reminding me that He has laid a task on my heart that I have not yet finished. Often, we can let other good stuff get in the way of the best stuff God has to offer. Dig into verse 5 because the last eight words are powerful: "I will never leave you nor forsake you."

If you are facing an assignment and feeling frustrated or disappointed, it could be that you have deviated from God's original instructions. How are you spending your time? Could you be using a spiritual substitute or trying to take a shortcut?

People are on the quest for happiness and satisfaction. However, they often turn to the wrong thing to fulfill their void.

Look at Isaiah 55:8–9, two of my favorite verses in the Bible. I have often used these verses when counseling students. "'For my thoughts are not your thoughts, neither are your ways my ways,' declares the Lord. 'As the heavens are higher than the earth, so are my ways higher than your ways and my thoughts than your thoughts.'"

God's thoughts are higher, but our thoughts are weaker. God's ways are best, but ours can often be disastrous. God's plan is perfect, but ours are flawed.

As you spend time in God's Word, think about what He is calling you to do. It could be going on a mission trip, teaching a new class, financially sacrificing toward a project or goal, or ending a relationship that is spiritually weighing you down. The list could go on and on, but God's plan is concrete. He will show you, but you must come to Him with a willing heart and receptive spirit.

God also tells Joshua to "be strong and courageous." This command is stated four times. When God repeats a word or phrase, we need to pay attention. It reminds me of when I must tell my children something repeatedly. By the third or fourth time I have said it, they know it is serious.

What is the first thing that comes to mind when you hear the words strong and courageous? What images do you see?

_____
_____
_____
_____

I immediately think of my mom. If you saw a picture of her, you might be confused and wonder why those words would conjure up her image in my mind. She was a petite lady and a spiritually fierce warrior. You wanted her on your side or her knees battling for you.

I can remember my freshman year in college, twenty years ago. I moved into Furman University the same week my dad was admitted to the hospital for severe depression. I remember telling my mom I wanted to delay starting school to stay home with her. I could have easily started in January.

Mom looked at me and with her mom voice firmly told me I was not doing that. She said, "Your dad is going to be okay. God has completely provided for you to attend Furman. We know this is His will for your life. It is time for you to start that journey now, not to delay it."

I can remember standing on the curb as she pulled away. I was crying, and I know she was, too, but she never let me see her tears. She knew I would have packed my bags and headed back to Inman. She pulled out of the front gate of campus and drove the one-hour-and-fifteen-minutes trip back to our house. Being strong and courageous can look different in the various seasons of our lives.

God repeated His command to Joshua because He knew how tempting it would be for Joshua to give in to defeat and despair. It would have been easy to start following his own plan instead of relying on the Master's plan.

God is also calling you to be strong and courageous. Whatever the plan for your life, He will walk alongside you and be ahead of you, paving the way. The key is to obey His plan and not deviate from it. Remember that prosperity and success look different in God's eyes. Keep your heart and mind focused on His ways.

I challenge you to memorize Joshua 1:7–9. Write these verses on an index card, along with what God is calling you to do this year. Place this card where you will see it often. When Satan begins to attack (and he most certainly will), quote this verse. God will give you the same courage and strength that He gave my mom in September 1994 and Joshua hundreds of years ago. Claim it today.

Day Two
Faith at the Fountain

When Stephen and I first served in student ministry, we planned a family night at the local roller-skating rink. It was going well until they called everyone into the middle of the floor for the "hokey pokey." When the leader said, "Right foot in," Stephen lost his balance and fell. I was laughing at Stephen and then lost my balance and fell, too. The difference was I came down hard on my elbow, fracturing it. I had to wear a sling for six weeks. Whenever someone asked what happened, I wanted to tell them an incredible story, not one that started with, "Well, we were doing the hokey pokey." It generated a lot of laughs. I never hear those three words without remembering that incident.

Today, we will read about an amazing story of faith and courage. A time when a few men were given instructions to place their right foot in the middle of raging waters. Read Joshua 3.

Joshua instructed the men carrying the Ark of the Covenant to stand in the Jordan. "And as soon as the priests who carry the ark of the Lord — the Lord of all the earth — set foot in the Jordan, its waters flowing downstream will be cut off and stand up in a heap."

This was a defining moment in the life of Joshua's leadership and ministry. "And the Lord said to Joshua, 'Today I will begin to exalt you in the eyes of all Israel, so they may know that I am with you as I was with Moses'" (7).

"Today" is one powerful word. I wonder if Joshua asked any questions when God explained how He was going to stop the Jordan's flow. It didn't appear that he wavered or questioned God's tactics. He immediately explained to the children of Israel what God was calling them to do.

Close your eyes and imagine the sacred Ark of the Covenant being carried.

"Now the Jordan is at flood stage all during harvest. Yet as soon as the priests who carried the ark reached the Jordan and their feet touched the water's edge, the water from upstream stopped flowing" (15–16).

I can imagine the fear and thoughts racing through their minds.
- What if God doesn't do what He says He will do?
- What if we place our right foot in and get swept away?
- What if we lose the sacred ark?

Yet, as soon as they placed their feet in the water, it stopped flowing and stood still.
- Think about what waters are raging in your life right now.
- Where do you need to exhibit great faith?
- Are you hesitating to complete a task God has laid on your heart?

Pray that God would give you complete discernment about areas where you need to trust Him more.

When I was five, my mom was diagnosed with breast cancer. I remember coming home from kindergarten and seeing her sick from chemotherapy. She was only thirty-two when she heard, "Mrs. Hammett, your biopsy came back positive. You have cancer."

The word cancer carries so much weight. It absolutely frightens me. My doctor once said, "Julie, you are going to worry so much about getting cancer that you are going to die from a heart attack. Stop worrying. You cannot control it." Those last four words are scary for someone who thrives on an agenda and loves to create a plan.

The priests could not control the flood waters but had to do their part. They had to exhibit great faith to wade in the water. They had to trust that God would do what He said. God never fails. If He is calling you to something, He will see you through it.

When I was a little girl, I remember sitting through some powerful services at my home church, Grace Baptist, where my dad pastored. It was a church that was physically small, yet full of people who had faith and believed in the power of the Lord. On one occasion, my dad had led someone to the Lord before the service began. It was during this same time that my mom was battling cancer. She told me that while she was at the water fountain early that Sunday morning, the Lord directed her to Mark 2:9–11.

"Which is easier: to say to this paralyzed man, 'Your sins are forgiven,' or to say, 'Get up, take your mat and walk'? But I want you to know that the Son of Man

has authority on earth to forgive sins.' So he said to the man, 'I tell you, get up, take your mat and go home.'"

My mom had written on a card in her Bible, "I didn't know what to think at first, but I knew then that God was speaking to me. I knew we were about to have a powerful worship service, and we did. We had an amazing service that day. In the end, I felt led to go to the altar and pray. I looked up, and a sea of church family surrounded me, all praying for the miraculous. As my earthly father came to kneel and pray over me, I felt as though a hot poker ran through my body. It was unlike anything I had ever experienced. I knew that the Lord had healed my body of cancer, even before the doctor confirmed it to be true."

One week later, my mom went to the doctor, and her scan was cancer free. The doctors were stunned. Our family was not. I have often wondered what would have happened if my mom had allowed fear or insecurity to keep her from going to the altar that morning. I was blessed to have my mom for thirty-one additional years. She exhibited faith at the fountain, and I know I will see her one day. Even as I type this, I believe she is in heaven, sitting by a brook of water that never runs dry.

Think about where you need to exhibit great faith. It could be with your children, finances, or marriage. It might mean taking a leap of faith and signing up for a mission trip or funding someone else's trip. God will show you, and He will provide. The uneasy part will be placing your right foot in as you wait on His timing to still the waters. If He is calling you to it, He will work in and through you to accomplish His will.

Day Three
Thirty-Seven Is a Good Age

On every birthday, from the time I was six, my mom would give me a birthday card that said, "Six is a good age." Then, "Seven is a good age." When I was five, Mom was diagnosed with cancer. She was debilitated in so many ways from the chemotherapy and radiation that she treasured every moment she could enjoy. She would always say, "Enjoy this year. You will only be this age once." I did not understand and appreciate this until I got older and reached the double digits. I was blessed to have thirty-six birthdays with my precious mom.

The year after my mom died, I dreaded my birthday. She always went out of her way to make birthdays special and, in her own way, over the top. We never had a lot of money, but I always felt cherished and celebrated. After my mom died, my oldest daughter, Natalie, realized I was struggling. As much as she missed her grandmother, she knew I was deeply grieving my mom.

On the morning of my thirty-seventh birthday, I put on the best happy face I could as I opened presents from my husband and children before we left for school. It was hard to put one foot in front of the other. When I climbed into the car to drive to school, I saw a huge handmade card attached to the steering wheel. On the cover, it said, "Thirty-seven is a good age to be." Natalie had made this card and placed it in my car the night before my birthday. It was such a sweet reminder not to wallow in the past but to fully live in the present.

Moments are fleeting, and we need to capture as many as possible. We cannot thrive in the way God intended for us if we allow ourselves to be defined by our worst number or date. On this birthday, I was allowing September 2012 — the date my mom died — to monopolize my thoughts and affect my attitude.

God will supply you with grace and peace that can only come from His infinite supply. I never fully grasped this until I experienced it for myself. God used that card from Natalie to remind me I was surviving, not thriving. That is certainly not God's plan for us.

Fast forward to December 2014. I was saying my earthly goodbye to my dad, thirty minutes before he died. I remember telling him he would soon be joining Mom in heaven. I said, "Dad, when you see her, tell her how much we miss her and tell her all about Ruthie."

My youngest daughter, Ruthie, was born two years after my mom died. Mom never got to meet and spoil her. At the time, Dad could not speak, but he nodded his head. He had told me a month earlier how much he would miss watching Ruthie grow up.

I was drowning again in the abyss of grief, reliving losing Mom and facing the reality that Dad would soon be gone as well. I was not ready or willing to face a life without either parent. Dad died later that day, and living without either parent became a stark reality. I wept. I yelled. I then had to face telling my precious children they had lost their grandfather.

Even as I type this six years later, it is still a moment and time Satan can use to form bitter thoughts in my mind. Satan can use this against me when he makes me doubt and question why I must live without my precious, godly parents. Do not live there. Do not camp out and put up stakes in that sea of grief. The waves will pull you under, and before you know it, your current number will be swallowed up by a number in the past. God brought me back to Isaiah 43.

"Forget the former things; do not dwell on the past. See I am doing a new thing! Now it springs up; do you not perceive it? I am making a way in the wilderness and streams in the wasteland. The wild animals honor me, the jackals and the owls, because I provide water in the wilderness and streams in the wasteland, to give drink to my people, my chosen" (Isaiah 43:18–20).

A way in the wilderness. That was what I needed desperately. When my children have a babysitter, we often come home to find they have built a fort. It is one of their favorite activities. Pillows, blankets, and stuffed animals have been transformed into a protective covering for their sneak attacks. Those attacks consist of anything from laser tag to Nerf wars to good old-fashioned hide-n-seek. We often come home to a collective sigh and this statement: "Are you already back? Why didn't you stay out longer?" So nice to be missed.

One day, I asked Tyler and Ruthie what was so special about these forts that they enjoyed building. Tyler said, "Well, they just make you feel safe. You can decide what you let in and protect against the rest." As I prepared for this study guide, the Lord brought me back to that statement from my then-eight-year-old.

Today, you are going to dig into Joshua 6. Before you read this passage, list areas in your individual, married, and family life where you feel as though you are being attacked. Where is it that Satan is aiming his fiery darts? What areas specifically need protecting?

_____

_____

_____

Spend some time in prayer, asking for God's protection over the above areas, and then read Joshua 6.

What a powerful passage of Scripture. Notice God's instructions in these verses. For six days, the people were to march around the city one time every day with armed men. On the seventh day, they were to march around seven times, blow their trumpets, and give a loud shout. The walls would come tumbling down (3–5). I don't know about you, but if I were going to inhabit a city, I would question that strategy of attacking the place. I would want some shinier tactics involving weapons and sneak attacks instead of visibly marching around the city.

Notice in verse 6 that Joshua did not hesitate. He immediately put into place God's instructions.

"And he ordered the army, 'Advance! March around the city, with an armed guard going ahead of the ark of the Lord'" (6:7).

No delay. No hesitation. No questioning. No asking, "What if?" This way, the Lord would receive all the credit, honor, and glory. No one would wonder how it happened because only God could accomplish such a feat.

God impressed four words on my heart as I prepared this devotion:
- **Respond**
- **Regard**

- **Recover**
- **Rebuild**

Respond
- How are you responding to what God is calling you to do?
- Is their hesitation and delay or willing obedience? At a seminar at The Cove, I heard Richard Blackaby say, "Delayed obedience is simply just disobedience."
- Does God have to ask only once before you comply? Are you saying yes to whatever He is calling you to do, even if you don't quite understand the instructions?

Regard

"But keep away from the devoted things so that you will not bring about your own destruction by taking any of them. Otherwise, you will make the camp of Israel liable to destruction and bring trouble on it" (Joshua 6:18).

Consider what areas and devoted things you need a hedge of protection against. You must actively guard against what the world tells you defines success.
- Are you communicating more with a co-worker than your spouse?
- Have you allowed social media to infiltrate your home? Are their applications that need to be deleted from your phone or your teenager's phone?
- Are finances and material possessions dominating your life?

- Do you feel as though you never have enough time and that you are constantly running? Satan loves to keep us busy and distracted with the devoted things so that we won't accomplish God's objectives.

The above are just a few I often hear as a counselor for parents and teenagers.

Finally, once you know where the gaps are, you need to recover and rebuild.

The first few words in verse 21 say, "They devoted the city to the Lord." Such powerful words. Can the Lord say the same thing about you, your marriage, and your family?

One Christmas, I had to decide to choose presence over absence. It seemed that everywhere I looked, I was reminded that my parents were no longer here. From hanging my childhood ornaments on the tree to uncovering a Santa house my mom and I had painted together, tears would flow. I miss my parents every day. However, Christmas is such a special time of year. The grief can surge like a tidal wave and sometimes feel as if it is pulling me under. I would liken it to an undertow experienced on a beach.

Undertow is defined as when a "broken wave pushes water up the beach, and gravity pulls the water back down the beach as backwash. When big waves break on the beach, a large uprush and backwash of water and sand are generated; this seaward-flowing water/sand mixture is pulled strongly into the next breaking wave. Beachgoers feel as if they are being pulled underwater when the wave breaks over their head — this is undertow."

Pulled under. I couldn't describe the ebb and flow of grief any better than those two words. For me, I had to recover and rebuild by focusing on who was here instead of who was missing. Presence versus absence. Maybe that is a picture of your life. Instead of focusing on your worst day and allowing that to define you, rebuild your foundation on the solid rock.

The challenges for today are listed below:
- **Respond** — Say yes to whatever God is calling you to do. Pray, "Yes, Lord, today."
- **Regard** — Are your devoted things ruling and reigning?
- **Recover and Rebuild** — Don't let Satan pull you under with the wreckage of grief, divorce, or depression. Ask God to focus you on His presence versus the absence of who or what you are so desperately missing.

The first few words of verse 27 say, "So the Lord was with Joshua." That needs to be our prayer and focus above any other — that we could proclaim, "So the Lord was with _____ (your name here). So the Lord was with _____ _____ (your children's names). So the Lord was with your family."

Day Four
Two Months at Best

I am writing today's devotional using my dad's Bible. He would have been seventy-five. I often read his Bible and looked at the tattered sermons between the pages. I think about the days when he faithfully brought God's Word and when he was so weak from the cancer attack on his body.

After my mom died, I thought my dad would have lived for at least twenty more years. However, that was not God's plan. On the morning of what would have been his seventy-fourth birthday, I couldn't sleep. God woke me up at four in the morning with the word for today's devotional.

God impressed me with the following words: "Julie, so many people are talking about a church experience lately when they need a real encounter with the living one. Your dad knew the difference. Continue to lead people to the only one who can change their lives."

Experience vs. Encounter — In today's study guide, you will examine those two words as they apply to your life and those around you as you relinquish the number holding you back from all that God intended you to be.

Read Matthew 26:36–46. The Garden of Gethsemane was one of my favorite places when I journeyed to Israel in 2019. Jesus took Peter, James, and John with Him and left the others behind. When He returned, He found the other disciples asleep. They were missing this encounter with the one and only Jesus, who would soon be nailed to a cross.

Jesus said, "Watch and pray so that you will not fall into temptation. The spirit is willing, but the flesh is weak" (Matthew 26:41).

A weak flesh is something I can relate to in different seasons of life. When my daughter Ruthie was five months old, I was struggling. It seemed there was always something to claim my attention. Three children had sent our world into overdrive. Laundry, bottles, diapers, homework, and lunches to pack were just a few of the daily tasks that overwhelmed me. In those moments, I began to wonder who created the theory behind the six- to twelve-week maternity leave. That is not nearly enough time to recover physically, spiritually, and emotionally from bringing a new life into the world.

During this time, I also received a phone call from my dad's doctor while I was at work. He told me my dad's recent PET scan results were not good. His exact words were, "Sam's melanoma has spread everywhere. I am surprised. We thought we got all of it. I am calling to prepare you for tomorrow when you bring your dad to his appointment. Let us deliver the news. Julie, I just wanted you to know before you come tomorrow so that you could prepare."

I had previously worked with this physician and will be forever grateful for that phone call. God was working in that phone call to prepare my heart and mind for what was to come. Six months prior, my dad had skin cancer removed from his back. In just that short of a window, it had spread everywhere.

The next day, when the doctor delivered the news to my dad, he said, "Mr. Hammett, the cancer has spread to your bones, liver, and spleen. You have two months at best, even with treatment." Those are words that are forever etched in my memory. It was one of those moments when the room started spinning, and everything became fuzzy. The doctor continued to talk. However, his words had lost their meaning. It was almost as if he was speaking in another language. Tears filled my eyes and streamed down my face. We had just lost my mom two years before. I felt as though I was in the middle of a bad dream.

In those moments, you want the experience to be different. You want the number to be so much greater. Dad seemed stoic. He was definitely handling it better than Stephen and me until he saw Ruthie. As tears streamed down his face, I knew what he was thinking. He would not get to invest in her and watch her grow up.

Dad was diagnosed on October 9 and went home to be with the Lord on December 11. It was a fast two months. I know God granted me the precious gift of time to say goodbye. I thought I was doing well because I was going from one thing to the next. It was easier for me to go, go, go instead of taking time to deal — to survive from one day to the next. This is ironic because, as a school counselor, I know that is not what I am supposed to do.

I was angry and needed the Lord more than I ever had. It was another night that I couldn't sleep and got up to pray in the living room. I felt forsaken.

God spoke to me so clearly. I wrote His words in my journal. Anytime God speaks, write it down so you can go back and claim it when you need to.

Julie, I have not forsaken you. You are my child. I am going to take care of your dad so that he will not suffer. He is my child. Enjoy these last days with him. They are a gift. I have plans for Natalie, Tyler, and Ruthie. As you prepare to move, I will provide for your job as I've always provided. However, it will be different this time — not in a way you expect. Your mom is doing well. She is ready to welcome your dad home. You need to finish the work I have called you to do. I have not forsaken you. Now, go and sleep in peace.

This experience left me wanting to know more. You never want a genuine encounter with the Lord to end. Aren't you thankful for a heavenly Father who takes the time to care for and speak to His children?

Those days were a gift of time. My dad had been diagnosed with the initial stages of dementia before his melanoma. During those two months, God cured him of those mental lapses. He was sharper than Stephen and me when the doctors and nurses asked him questions.

An experience is fleeting; an encounter is forever.

An experience is easily forgotten; an encounter is engrained in your memory.

Spend some time in prayer and ask yourself the following questions:
- Have you had an encounter with the living one, or are you just surviving from experience to experience? Are you asleep in the garden, or are you walking alongside Jesus like Peter, James, and John? Would Jesus have called your name?
- Who do you know that needs to have an encounter with the living one? Draw a prayer circle around the names that God lays on your heart. It is not if but who God will impress upon you.

Everyone knows someone needing an encounter with the only one with the power to change his or her life.

Day Five
Drinking the Cup

I enjoy collecting coffee mugs from places I have traveled. I especially love the memories they conjure when I retrieve one from the cabinet. I have some mugs that my children have hand painted over the years and some that I bought at different destinations. When Stephen has gone on a trip, he often has brought one back for me. But it is not the same when I have not been to that place myself. I love receiving it, but there are no emotional ties to it. No memories.

This week, take a trip across the Kidron Valley to a garden. The disciples are there. Jesus is there. I want you to imagine yourself there. Judas Iscariot is there and makes a pre-meditated decision that will forever change his life. An opportunity came for him to take a stand with Jesus of Nazareth, but he betrayed him instead (John 18:2–3). Judas was given the same opportunity as Peter, James, and John, yet wasted it. A missed opportunity.

I do not have many regrets, but a missed opportunity is one of my greatest ones. I was introduced to the brevity of life at a young age. Since I was young when my mom was diagnosed with cancer, I grew up realizing the importance of every moment.

We are not guaranteed a long life, so we should make each second count. However, I do have one regret that I think about often. When Stephen and I were newlyweds, my dad was going on his third trip to Israel and wanted us to go with him. We had been married less than a year and were each working both secular and church jobs. Stephen was with an insurance company, and I was at the hospital. Additionally, we both served at a local church. I told myself I could not take off work for that long. It was the sensible choice, but one I have regretted since — a missed opportunity for me to share those memories with my dad.

One of my favorite photos of my dad is of him coming out of the empty tomb. You can see the grin on his face and sense the knowledge in his heart that Jesus had risen. Now, Dad is in heaven with that grin as he praises the Lord with other of my family members.

When you reflect on your life, what missed opportunities come to mind? Spend time reflecting and then pray that God would speak to you through today's Scripture.

___

Read John 18–19:6

Missed Opportunity #1 — Judas Iscariot

John 18:2 breaks my heart. I am crying now as I type this because I would hate to be referred to as "Now, Julie, who betrayed Him." Judas had walked with Jesus, broke bread with Him, and experienced the most intimate moments with Jesus. He had a front-row seat to the miracles Jesus performed.

I have often wondered when Judas decided to switch sides. We can speculate on when his heart changed, yet I want you to examine your heart today. Betrayal is never harder than when it comes from someone you love — from the person who is the closest to you. I have experienced that heartbreak before and am weeping as I think about Jesus' betrayal. Judas brings an army of folks with lanterns, weapons, and torches on a hunt to capture the King of Kings. Judas thought it was quite the plan. But he failed to recognize this was part of the master plan.

"Jesus commanded Peter, 'Put your sword away! Shall I not drink the cup the Father has given me?'" (John 18:11).

Drink the cup. It was time. One that Jesus didn't want to see pass. Aren't you thankful Jesus went to that old, rugged cross for us? For every sin we have or will ever commit, He was beaten and bruised. As I write this, this realization is heavy.

Take some time and thank the Lord for drinking the cup for your sins, for your children, and for your family.

Missed Opportunity #2 — Peter

Peter is one of my favorite biblical characters. He makes many mistakes yet continues to receive the forgiving grace of the Lord, time and time again.

Notice that Peter is standing outside the door when questioned about his relationship with Jesus. This is the first time he denies Jesus (John 18:16–17). It is a missed opportunity to recognize his affiliation with Jesus. Even at this moment, Peter is distancing himself.

They had to bring him into the room.

It is easy to cast stones at Peter, yet how often have we done the same thing? Peter crucified Jesus here on his own by denying Him. I have often missed chances to be bold in my faith out of fear of rejection or failure. After Peter denied Jesus, he began keeping company with the other side. One wrong choice led to another.

"It was cold, and the servants and officials stood around a fire they had made to keep warm. Peter also was standing with them, warming himself" (John 18:18).

This is the same disciple who walked on water to Jesus in Matthew 14:29. As I am writing this guide, God is pricking my heart with the conviction to be bolder. Sometimes, I hide behind the mask of being the pastor's wife. In my chaotic mind, everyone should already know I desire for them to have a relationship with the Lord.

I once asked a student, "If I went to your school and asked those who know you best to describe you in three words, what would they say? Would Christian be one of those words? Do they know you are associated with the risen King? This week, ask yourself that question about those you work with, play sports with, or coach with. Who would they say you are?

At one church where Stephen and I served, one girl broke my heart. I was her third-grade Vacation Bible School teacher. I had just finished giving the plan of salvation when she raised her hand, signifying she was not saved.

When I sat with her, she said, "I don't think I want to get saved. I can't figure it out.

My mom and dad come to church every Sunday and act one way and then go home, drink, curse, and yell at each other. Why should I want what they have?"

I was stunned. We sat in silence for a moment. I didn't know what to say. What she saw was fake religion. She did not see a real relationship with the Lord. That young lady is now in college and, to my knowledge, still has no relationship with the Lord.

For those of you who have children, you know they know you best. Would they want what you have? Would you want them to have your relationship with the Lord? Are you missing opportunities to show them your love for the Lord?

Are you like Peter? Are you standing outside the door trying to go unnoticed? At work? On your athletic team? At school? In your family?

Don't miss opportunities this week to reach those around you.

Week Four
Simplified and Sure

As we begin week four of this study, I hope you have been blessed. This last section will focus on the numbers that matter to God. This section will focus on making intentional investments in our sphere of influence. Take some time to examine your roots. God has continually reminded me there is much need for a root reset.

The word roots means different things to many people. Whether it is physical tree roots, graying hair roots (much like mine lately), or spiritual roots, the best roots are strong and healthy, with the ability to sustain the most powerful storm.

My thoughts about spiritual roots immediately run to two godly sets of grandparents. One who lived on a farm and one who lived right next door to my house as I was growing up. Both always made time for me when I would visit. One was often shucking corn outside, while the other was listening to Christian radio or watching *Wheel of Fortune*, depending on the time of day. The one thing they had in common was deep roots — legacies of abiding and dwelling in the Lord.

God whispered to me, "What if the root systems that are being developed today are shallow and weak? What if some need replanting?"

Paul wrote, "So that Christ may dwell in your hearts through faith. And I pray that you, being rooted and established in love, may have power, together with all the Lord's holy people, to grasp how wide and long and high and deep is the love of Christ" (Ephesians 3:17–18).

I thought of my three children and the type of roots my husband and I are putting down. God reminded me I needed to make intentional investments. As you begin this week, take some time to examine your root structure.

- **Redeem the Time**

As a busy mom of a fifteen-, eleven-, and six-year-old, our house is often chaotic. One may be playing basketball on the small hoop over his door while another is playing the guitar, while the other is teaching her class of twenty baby dolls and placing many of them in the "stinky square" because they were misbehaving.

I thought, *Lord, how will I manage this for multiple days?* He impressed upon my heart, "Julie, you will not have this day again. Use it wisely."

Have the conversation with your teenager you have been meaning to have. Play a game of basketball with your son that you never have the time to do. Join your five-year-old's imaginary class and relax. I hope she doesn't send me to the stinky square. Strengthen those roots with time management.

- **Order Your Steps**

Our kids watch every comment and step we make. Where do they lead? To the spiritual or superficial? My mom died before her dad. I knew she would have wanted a particular verse shared at his funeral: "The Lord makes firm the steps of the one who delights in him" (Psalm 37:23).

Papa Carter's steps were always faithful. He read his Bible daily, loved his family, and never spoke a harsh word about anyone. His steps were significantly affected by how he grew up. He always walked behind me — turning off the lights as I exited a room — ate every bit of food on his plate, and never thought about missing a church service for any other reason than sickness. He often talked about how the great recession of his time affected him. His steps impacted those who came behind him.

Spend some time thinking about where you are leading those who are following closely behind.

- **Orchestrate a Break from Social Media**

This one is difficult for me. I love connecting with others. However, God impressed on my heart that strong roots are not formed during screen time. They are formed with conversations and laughter. They are made in the messy moments of life. Those roots are made stronger even through the disagreements and frustrations of life. They will run deeper and sustain us during the hard times of life. The Lord has continued to remind me not to spend endless time watching what others are doing, while neglecting to connect with the ones under my roof.

- **Train the Littles**

During my COVID-19 attempt to homeschool, I was reminded that I never was good at math. I absolutely do not know how to navigate helping a five- and ten-year-old well. I get easily frustrated, which I never would with someone else's child. But just as we have to teach math, reading, and sight words, we have to teach them how to read their Bible, pray, and keep a journal. Let them learn from each other. Be intentional. Take this time to go deeper with them about hearing from the Lord. Put this first each day.

- **Simple and Strong**

During uncertain and changing times, trust that God has your best in mind. He is a loving Father who desires to give your family so much more. He wants you to grow and multiply many simple, strong, and deep roots. You must avoid the constant comparisons about what others are doing. Let them focus on their number while you focus on your own.

I pray that your family will experience Ephesians 3:18-19: "To grasp how wide and long and high and deep is the love of Christ, and to know this love that surpasses knowledge — that you may be filled to the measure of all the fullness of God."

During this week, focus on what you can accomplish in God's strength. Dig deep. Go farther. Examine your root structure. Multiply your number of roots.

Pathway to Freedom
$\infty + 0 + 1 = \text{MTJAN}$

Day One
Fleeing or Following: A Thousand Times No

As you begin week four, I want you to search your heart and ask yourself the following questions:

- Where are you making progress on your "number?" Celebrate the victories. Satan will have you focus on the defeat. You are in God's Word today seeking Him. Praise the Lord this morning.
- Have you ever felt God calling you to do something you did not want to do?
- When was the last time you received an answer you did not expect from someone?
- Have you felt yourself restless and wandering with disobeying the Lord's will?

God calls, and your reply is full of reluctance and reservation. The definition of reluctance is the "unwillingness to do something or lack of eagerness or willingness."

Read Jonah 1, but before you do, spend some time in prayer. Ask the Lord to show you if there is any area in your life where you are unwilling to follow His call. It could range from giving up a website or a particular genre of music to teaching a class, going on a mission trip, or serving where you sense God is leading.

If you are listening to God's voice, He will direct you. The challenge for this week is to say yes when He does.

Jonah did not want to follow the word that the Lord had given him. I did a little research and found that Tarshish stood more than 2,500 miles from Israel, in the opposite direction of Nineveh. It was the most remote destination available for Jonah to escape God's call. He did not want to go and minister to the Assyrians.

> *"But Jonah ran away from the LORD and headed for Tarshish. He went down to Joppa, where he found a ship bound for that port. After the fare, he went aboard and sailed for Tarshish to flee from the LORD"* (Jonah 1:3).

The English Standard Version of the Bible says, "From the presence of the LORD." "From the presence of the LORD" are six powerful words. I don't know about you, but they make me uncomfortable. The presence of the Lord should be something we want to partake in and draw closer to, not run away from. Jonah thought he could board that boat, hunker down in the lowest part of the ship, and sleep off this assignment (5). He was escaping. The fact that he went to the lowest part of the ship tells a story in itself.

My dad answered the call to ministry, but not before he ran for over a year. I heard him share this part of his testimony many times. My mom and dad were married when they were in their early twenties. Dad worked as a mechanic, and my mom worked as an administrative assistant. They were volunteering in a local church yet did not plan to work full-time in the ministry. The Lord began working in my dad's heart and life. He would say, "The Lord clearly called me to the ministry, and my answer was a resounding no. A thousand times I said no."

Dad did not share this call with anyone. He just continued to work. I remember him saying, "I thought if I just went on with my life as normal that God would call someone else. I did not think I was qualified to serve the Lord as a pastor."

But the Lord continued to speak to my dad, even though he said no. One morning, the Lord spoke to my dad and told him that his time to accept the call was coming to an end. My dad went to work that day with a heavy burden.

If you have ever run from the Lord, no matter what the call, it is a miserable experience. That day, as my dad worked maintenance on a large truck, an explosion occurred. He suffered third-degree burns and was transported to a burn center two hours away. He would often show a photo when he shared this story — a picture of him sitting in the burn unit, completely covered with the physical evidence of what it looks like to spiritually disobey God's call. He knew this was his "Tarshish" experience.

My dad recovered from his intense burns and surrendered to the call to ministry. He faithfully pastored for thirty-two years. I vividly remember him talking about the one-and-a-half years he ran from the call. He told me a month before he died that he was ready to meet the Lord and reunite with my mom: "Julie, I know I will have to answer for the time when I ran from God. I have always wondered how much blood will be on my hands for those I was supposed to lead to the Lord when I was too busy running the other direction."

My dad was a faithful servant for a long time. However, that period when he tried to hide from God's call underneath the hood of a truck always bothered him. It should bother us, too, when we deliberately disobey what God is asking.

Have you ever tried to run from the presence of the Lord? If so, what was the outcome?

The lack of fear and respect in our current society for authority continues to amaze me. We should all stand in awe of the God of the universe. The men on this ship were so afraid of the Lord that they picked Jonah up and threw him overboard to calm the raging sea (15). The following verse says, "At this the men greatly feared the Lord."

We should all have a holy reverence for the God we serve. We should teach that to our children, grandchildren, teenagers, and anyone God grants us the privilege and ability to invest in.

We could make guesses as to what initially made Jonah run. Fear? Comfort? Lack of control? Disregard for God's chosen audience for the message? Perhaps he wanted a different assignment. The Lord came to Jonah and said to get up, and in the next verse, Jonah did get up, but not to answer the call (2–3).

I wonder if Jonah thought about changing his mind during those two verses. How many thoughts ran through his mind as he stepped onto the ship and headed in the wrong direction? He knew his actions would adversely affect those around him, yet he did it anyway.

How often do we do the same thing? There have been many times when I have chosen my way over God's way. My plan over His.

The message for today is simple. As you close your time with the Lord, ask yourself the questions below. God certainly stepped on my toes in preparation for this devotion.

- Is God giving you a particular assignment? If so, are you fleeing or following His command?
- Are you saying yes or telling God a thousand times, "No, I will not follow You?"

We can try to make it sound better by quoting why we can't do what God asks. The following are some I often hear when someone is wrestling with a call from the Lord:

- "I can do that later. I am not sure I am ready now."
- "I just don't think it is the right time."
- "To follow His call, I will have to give up so much. I may have to move or sell my house."
- "How will this affect my family?"
- "What if …" You can finish that sentence. We have all asked a million "What if" questions.

No matter our reasoning, a no is just a no. If God is calling you, He wants you to do it, not another person. God will never call you to a task for you to suggest it to someone else. If He wanted them to do it, He would have given them the instructions.

The choice is yours to invest where your number of days will make a difference.

Day Two
When Christ Calls Your Name

When I was pregnant, I was frequently asked many questions and often by strangers. At times, it would feel like the great inquisition.

Questions would typically go in this order:

- When is your baby due?
- May I touch your belly?
- Are you having a boy or a girl?
- Are you having twins (my least favorite)?
- Have you picked out a name?

It would always amaze me when I would share the names we were considering, and people we didn't know well would share why we shouldn't choose those names.

Stephen and I always made a list of our favorite names and took long consideration into making our choice. A name is permanent. It is the first gift we bestow upon our precious little ones. It is one that we spend a lot of time calling and sometimes yelling.

As you continue your journey, read John 20. Imagine the Lord calling your name as He did Mary in verse 16. What stands out to you as you reflect on this passage?

How precious is it when the risen Christ calls our name? When He speaks, all doubt, fear, and uncertainty are replaced with assurance, faith, and knowing that He knows us by name.

First, notice Mary did not initially recognize who Jesus was. She thought He was the gardener. Not until He spoke her name did she realize whom she was speaking with (15–16).

As I was writing today's devotional, Christ gave me the following questions:

- Are you aware of when Christ is nearby?
- Do you sense His presence working in your heart and life?
- Do your children and grandchildren know how to recognize when He is at work?

I wrote today's devotion during the week leading to Easter. Growing up a pastor's kid, I never understood the new dresses, Easter baskets, gifts, and candy. We had those things, but as a young girl, I could not figure out why Easter was more special than any other day of the year. The same King who victoriously arose on Easter Sunday is the same one who lives the week after and the week after and the week after that.

I have a friend who told me that her brother likes the appearance of Easter. I didn't understand what she meant. She explained, "Well, his family will get dressed up, take pictures, and act as though they go to worship. But after the pictures, they put on jeans and go to eat lunch. It is important to our parents that they at least go on Easter. So, they take the photos."

This perplexed me. Why go to such trouble to please people when Christ knows our heart and name?

My name was called in a different way one year. Normal, routine, and expected are three words I often take for granted. I frequently complain the most during the mundane. I was reminded how ordinary moments can be the ones that are the most extraordinary. They are also the ones that are most missed when they are gone.

I had gone for a routine doctor's visit. The doctor found a place that looked suspicious. He diagnosed it as a subcutaneous nodule and referred me to an orthopedic surgeon. I saw this surgeon a few days later. He took an X-ray and said, "Mrs. Cannon, this is a lump, and it will have to be removed."

The doctor had been a surgeon for forty-one years. He thought it was benign but would need to be biopsied upon removal. This was on a Monday. My CT scan had been set up for the following Monday and then a visit with a specialist for the following Thursday. I called and had my CT scan moved from Spartanburg to the Village at Pelham.

When my doctor called to check on me, I explained that I had moved my scan to a different location. He volunteered to call the specialist to see if she could see me any sooner.

He called me back within minutes and said, "This is amazing. The same day you moved your scan to is the first day she will be seeing patients in that same location. You will be in the same building."

It was not a coincidence; it was all God. Even in the small details, He knows our name. The doctor told me he and the surgeon had consulted and thought this was a sacral tumor. I received this news before church on a Wednesday night and struggled to put one foot in front of the other.

As I sat in the waiting room at the doctor's office, I anxiously waited for the nurse to call my name. As I lay down for the CT scan, I looked up and saw my name on the machine above me. As tears streamed down my face during the scan, I was reminded that no matter the outcome, God knows my name. It was written so clearly on this machine.

As the machine took the images, all I could think of was my children. The moments I often complain about — packing lunches, the laundry, toys all over the house. How that, in a day, life can surely change with the outcome of one test. As soon as I left, my name disappeared, and the board reflected another name for another scan.

The verses God had given me for this week were Isaiah 43:1–2.

At the end of verse 1, it says, "Do not fear, for I have redeemed you; I have summoned you by name; you are mine."

When Stephen and I saw the specialist an hour later, she said she was confused. She showed us the CT images and said there was nothing there. The tumor that had been there a few days before was no longer showing on these new images. She was puzzled, but Stephen and I were not. We knew God had performed a miracle.

She said, "Mrs. Cannon, when your doctor called me yesterday, he was very concerned. Frankly, I thought we would be looking at surgery next week. However, there is nothing to operate on."

As I walked out of the waiting room that day, I was flooded with thoughts of thanksgiving.

- Thankful for another day to pack the children's lunches.
- Thankful for another day to wash the clothes and look for mismatched socks.
- Thankful for another day to sit in the car line.
- Thankful for another day to pick up Ruthie's baby dolls, which were strewn all over the house.

Just as God called Mary's name outside the empty tomb, He is calling your name today.

If you have surrendered your heart and life to the Lord, then you are His, as it says in Isaiah 43:1. If you are reading this and have never made that decision, what better time to make that choice?

I want to close today with Isaiah 43:2:

When you pass through the waters,
I will be with you;
and when you pass through the rivers,
they will not sweep over you.
When you walk through the fire,
you will not be burned;
the flames will not set you ablaze.

Everywhere it says "you," take a pen, cross it out, and write your name over the top. Personalize this verse to your life and family. Post it somewhere where you will see it often. I have it on my desk at work and look at it many times.

It doesn't say *if* we pass through the waters or walk through the fire. It says *when*. Beloved, you *will* pass through the waters, but you do not have to be afraid. You can relinquish control to the One who knows your name and number.

Day Three
On the Ninth Day of Christmas

I love everything about Christmas: the shiny ornaments, the bright Christmas lights, and the joy and expectation that accompanies the season. As you think about that magical time of year, list some of your favorite Christmas memories below.

_____
_____
_____
_____

Before you begin today, pray and ask God to speak to your heart and mind. Specifically, pray over those in your life whom you have the privilege of investing in — those whom you could shape their remembrances. If you have children or grandchildren, you do not have to look far to create that list. It could also be athletes whom you coach, children or teenagers whom you teach in school, or preschoolers whom you teach in Sunday school.

Create a list below, pray over those this morning, and then read Joshua 4.

_____
_____
_____

I have fond memories of one specific Christmas. It was when I had the blessing of viewing the magic of the season through the eyes of my precious three-year-old, Ruthie. That particular year, she loved singing loudly about baby Jesus in the manger, creating her long Christmas list (every other day), and getting excited when we drove by a house with a single strand of glowing lights. Her innocence and childlike faith amazed me.

Ruthie is our third and probably our final child, making every experience a little sweeter. The essence of time is valued more, for I remember when my sixteen- and twelve-year-old were that age. Their numbers are growing, so the amount of time I have to spend with them under our roof is lessening.

That Christmas season, Ruthie was out in what she called big church more often for family worship services and musicals. As we sat in the sanctuary, she propped herself on my lap and asked many questions.

Below are her questions, and in parentheses, you can see to what she was referring:

- "What are those shiny plates for?" (tithes and offering)
- "Is it time to eat that bread? Why are people lining up for that? What is in those little cups?" (communion)
- "Is it my time to sing? I know the "Twelve Days of Christmas." (At one point, she starts singing "On the Ninth Day of Christmas" repeatedly. For some reason, the ninth day was of great interest to her.)
- "Are we going to eat now? Can we go to Moe's?" (Apparently, seeing the bread and juice had made her hungry.)

- "Can I go and sit with Daddy?" (Daddy would be the pastor, and it was not a good time for her to sit with him at that particular moment. I distracted her with stickers and candy.)

Those are just a few, however. One question I heard quite often in each service that she attended that year was, "Do I have to be quiet? Why can't I talk now?"

I remember a sweet lady from one church where my husband pastored who said, "Julie, you will teach your children many things. One thing that also must be taught is sitting in a service. What does it all mean? Why should your children care about these things? They must learn and ask. As they age, they will not learn from sitting in a room in the back of the church. They will learn from watching you."

Ouch. Sweet Ms. Rita stepped on my spiritual toes with those words one night when I had taken our oldest daughter Natalie out of the service for talking.

So back to the question, "Do I have to be quiet now?"

I explained to her that at certain times she can talk, but at others, she needs to be quiet. She just looked at me. She was mulling over my words. During one service, I was worn out. I had gone through coloring books, stickers, candy, and suckers and got frustrated. The struggle in the pew with an active and inquisitive three-year-old was getting the best of me.

During this family candlelight Christmas service, the Lord spoke to me. We had reached the part where families lined up to take communion. The pastor would then pray over each family.

Ruthie immediately said, "I want to pray over at Daddy's table," and took off in that direction. When we approached the table, she didn't understand she could not help Daddy give out the bread. I wasn't sure the folks in line would appreciate her hands on the small pieces of bread, which represented Jesus' sacrifice for us.

Then, I heard the Lord, "Julie, remember her little hands and captive heart are exactly who I died for."

As Ruthie sat with me at the front, waiting for the line to dwindle, she grew increasingly impatient. She wanted to stand with her daddy. The pianist was playing "Silent Night" while families gathered together. It was quiet — a beautiful moment.

Suddenly, my three-year-old started crying loudly, "I don't understand. I want to go up there."

Reasoning with her had ended. The silent part of the night was over. I picked her up, and she went limp like a noodle. Honestly, I was angry as I walked back to my husband's office, where we would wait until the service ended.

The Lord convicted me. "Julie, be careful with exactly what you say."

Tears were streaming down her little face. She did not understand what was happening or why she could not be with her favored parent. She is a daddy's girl. God pricked my heart as He so often does. What we say in such moments can shape how our children view life. Ruthie's second home is the church. She is there three times a week without a choice in the matter.

However, the Lord reminded me, "Julie, one day she will have a choice. This is not a time to punish her, but to teach her. What do you want her to remember about tonight?"

As you think about the word, remember, reread Joshua 4:21–24. God instructed the people to take twelve stones to remind them how faithful the Lord was to provide what they needed when they needed it the most (6–7, 23–24).

The three words the Lord woke me up with at 4:15 that morning were the ones we will focus on: relate, refrain, remember.

Look back at the list you created before you began reading today — the list of people in your realm of influence. As you look at those names, think about these three.

The Lord knew that time would diminish the miraculous that had just occurred. In my Experiencing God Study Bible, it says, "The most profound encounters with the Lord can grow dim in our memory."

God wanted His people to have a visual reminder of His goodness and grace — not just for them but also for their children. We need teachable moments and spiritual markers. Our children need them, too.

Relate to your children and those in your sphere of influence. How is God working in and through your life? What spiritual markers are you leaving for them?

Refrain from punishing them, as I was about to do in Stephen's office, when it is a matter of shaping, teaching, and helping them to understand.

Remember, in five or ten years, you will want your children to remember about this season of life.

One thing is for sure: The above will not happen by accident. God gave clear instructions to His people in this passage, which apply today.

As you progress on your spiritual journey, focus on placing some spiritual markers as individuals, couples, and families that will surpass your life and memory.

Take time to create a list of spiritual markers where you have seen God clearly at work in your heart and life.

Day Four
Multitudes: Most or Mostest?

Large crowds are one of my least favorite things. I am mildly claustrophobic and often find myself looking for escape routes. When I think of large crowds, two places immediately come to mind: Disney World and the mall on Thanksgiving weekend.

When I was six months pregnant with Ruthie, Stephen and I took Natalie and Tyler to Disney. I am not sure why we thought that was a good idea. I am going to blame it on pregnancy hormones. At one point, we were in Magic Kingdom when they closed the park because it was full, as if we needed an announcement.

People were everywhere. I remember being in line for one of the stunt car shows and looking around at a sea of people. It was overwhelming, and since I was six months pregnant, I was mainly concerned about how to get more of those yummy ice cream bars and the location of the restrooms. I would not escape the multitude of people until I exited the park for the day.

As I read the Scripture for this week, the word multitude continued to draw me in and is one we will examine. Before we read our Scripture, ask yourself the following questions:

- Who would you say is in your crowd?
- Would your closest friends describe you as a leader or a follower?
- Are your decision-making abilities easily swayed by those around you?

The number of folks around us can be a blessing or a distraction. As you evaluate those in your multitude, pray for God's discernment and then read Matthew 21:1–11. In these verses, the word crowd is mentioned in verses 8, 9, and 11. In the New Kings James Version, the word "multitude" is used. This word is associated with the word "more," and often in our society that deems it to be better and/or more important.

My children love to use the word "more" frequently, especially when it relates to dessert. Recently, I overheard my son say, "I don't understand why Dad gets more ice cream than me." The response we usually give him is, "Dad is older and entitled to more."

Often in America, the word "more" is associated with being the best, when it can be the worst. More electronics, more money, more food, more hours at work, more text messages, and more emails, all of which can lead to an inward focus, distracted spirit, and a self-centered attitude.

The first area I want you to evaluate regards your multitude of people. Does your crowd draw you closer to the Lord or pull you further away? If Jesus were heading up your road, would you be in the sea of people wanting to catch a glimpse, or would you be at home catching the story on your smartphone?

The second multitude comes from Isaiah 1:11–17. Read these verses and think about a different type of multitude. In this passage, we see the word multitude in a slightly different context. As you search your heart and mind, think about multitude not only in terms of people but also in terms of sacrifice. Our stuff doesn't impress the Lord. He wants us. I often wonder how heartbroken my heavenly Father must be when I prioritize something else over Him.

> *"The multitude of your sacrifices — what are they to me?" says the LORD. "I have more than enough of burnt offerings, of rams, and the fat of fattened animals; I have no pleasure in the blood of bulls and lambs and goats" (Isaiah 1:11).*

In these verses, God tells His people that the multitude of sacrifices is unpleasing to Him. In the first part of verse 13, God says, "Stop bringing meaningless offerings." It is not the amount of sacrifice in God's eyes. The number is insignificant. The heart out of which you are giving is what is important.

As the Lord speaks into your heart and mind, how would He finish the sentence below? In my life, He could finish it in any one of the following ways.

"Julie, I have had enough of your procrastination, distractions, fear, anxiety, and worry." How is God speaking to you today? How would you fill in the blanks below?

_____

_____

_____

Hear God speak over your life: "You do not need a multitude of people or stuff; you only need to rely on and trust in me."

Since she was seven, my oldest daughter, Natalie, has loved the Samaritan's Purse shoebox ministry. At that age, she collected items for months until she had enough to make ten shoeboxes.

Natalie would easily talk my mom into helping her buy packs of crayons, socks, and hair bows to fill these boxes. I often remember her using some of her birthday money to buy some items. Her offering had meaning and substance. Her "more" meant something.

But one year, we had to teach her that her "more" was not coming from the right supply. She had collected many small toys. I couldn't imagine how she had enough money to fill several large containers of toys. Natalie smirked and told me that her younger brother had too much. He needed to clean out. She had just taken it upon herself to start that process. I explained to her that we could not give what was not ours to give.

Tyler agreed to give some of what she had gathered and then exclaimed, "I can give the mostest. I have a great idea." Natalie quickly informed him that "mostest" was not a word. He just rolled his eyes at his older sister and then proceeded to come back with about ten shirts in hand. "I am going to give all of my button-up shirts. They need them more than me!"

Oh, what a sacrifice he was willing to make. I had to explain to him that we don't give simply what we don't want to keep for ourselves. We give our best stuff.

My youngest daughter Ruthie will often say, "I love you." I will then answer her with, "I love you more." She then exclaims, "I love you mostest." I smile and think that must be how our heavenly Father feels about us. We can never out-give Him. He loves us the mostest.

If the Lord is the head and heartbeat of your multitude, you are on the right path. Press in and continue your journey to make less of yourself and your number and to make the mostest of Him.

Day Five
Rags to Riches

As I have shared, Stephen and I have three kids at three different ages in different seasons of life. It is overwhelming to me sometimes that the Lord chose me to be their mother. I have lots of days that teenagers would term epic fail. There are many moments when I wish I could have a second chance to get it right.

Today, we are going to study Proverbs 31. You may laugh a little. The words listed below are not typically heard in the day-to-day aspect of being a woman.

- Far above rubies (10)
- Girds herself with strength (17)
- Household clothed with scarlet (21)
- Strength and honor her clothing (25)
- Opens her mouth with wisdom and on her tongue is the law of kindness (26)

Let's be honest for a moment. How many times have we opened our mouths without kindness on our tongues? The moments in our house that are the most frantic are in the morning. Backpacks. Lunchboxes. Last minute homework review. Everything is done in a hurry to rush out the door at 7:10 a.m., so everyone can be where they need to be on time. Ruthie calls it the "hurry, scurry, Murray" moment. I'm unsure who Murray is, but the hurry and scurry are right.

Read Proverbs 31. As you do, list below the people who have richly impacted your life. Who are those people who have invested in you?

_____
_____
_____
_____

As you look at the above list, I am sure these people impacted your life because they abided in the Lord. You will dig a little deeper today as we study this passage of Scripture and how it relates to being the mother, daughter, niece, cousin, sister, grandmother, or aunt God has called you to be.

I took each letter of the word abide and made an acrostic. Pray that God will show you which letter He would have you focus on this week.

Abundant Life

God wants us to live a life that is abundant and full. To do that, we might have to rid ourselves of distractions that keep us from being all God has called us to be. Spend a few minutes asking the Lord if there is an area where you need to scale back. Is there an application on your phone that you need to delete? Is there an unhealthy relationship that needs to end? The definition of abundant is "existing in large quantities, plentiful."

Abundance also means "rich, lavish, generous, overflowing, and ample." Do these words describe your spiritual life, or would you describe it as depleted, empty, and defeated? To abide in Him and experience his abundance, you have to be willing to focus on the best that He has to offer. There are a lot of good things that will demand your attention. The question is where does God want you to focus?

Binds Her Tongue (8, 26)

I researched this one week and found that the average woman speaks twenty-thousand words daily, while the average man speaks seven thousand. I am probably well above average in this category. "She speaks with wisdom, and faithful instruction is on her tongue" (Proverbs 31:26).

Once our words come out of our mouths or are posted on social media, we cannot retrieve them. I remember my fourth-grade Sunday school teacher explaining the above verse with a tube of toothpaste. She squirted a whole tube of toothpaste onto a plate and then asked us to place it back in the tube. We couldn't complete that task.

It is the same way with our spoken words. Think about what words are oozing from your mouth. What you are sharing with your children. What are you posting on social media? Does it glorify the Lord? Ask the Lord to show you how to be more faithful in your instruction. Also, ask Him to give you wisdom and discernment when it comes to being the woman, man, mother, father, grandmother, or grandfather He wants you to be.

In His Strength (17)

Verse 17 says, "Her arms are strong for her task." To be the woman God calls you to be, you must do it in His strength, not your own. I heard something once about parenting I have never forgotten: The goal should be for your children to move from dependence on you to dependence on God.

How would you rate yourself on teaching your children, grandchildren, or nieces/nephews to rely on the Lord? Satan loves when you gird yourself in your strength. He knows when He can get you to accomplish something on your own, that most times, it will fail miserably.

In His strength, not in _____ (write your name) strength. Go back and review Isaiah 41:10 from a few weeks ago. It is one of my favorites.

Dressed in Riches (21–22, 25)

In these verses, you will find several words relating to how you should dress: scarlet, fine linen, purple, strength, and honor. Do these words describe your spiritual wardrobe? I admitted a few weeks ago that I love to shop. I always tend to gravitate toward the same style and dress color when shopping. Stephen says, "That looks like one you already have." Honestly, I tend to buy it anyway if I like it. I do have a lot of outfits in the same color. God reminded me that we also often get comfortable and gravitate toward a similar pattern in our relationship with Him.

Think about your spiritual wardrobe. Does it look pristine while you are spiritually dressed in tattered rags? Are you falling apart on the inside when you have access to fine linen and royal purple garments in Christ? God wants to take you this week from rags to the riches He offers. Are you willing? It demands a sacrifice.

Extends Equipping Grace (20)

This verse talks about extending a hand to those in need. For a moment, think about how Jesus invested in His disciples. He lived with them, taught them, instructed them, fished with them, and traveled with them. Although Jesus ministered to and loved on the masses of people who followed Him, He primarily devoted Himself to the work of a few so that the masses may be reached more effectively.

His number was smaller here. He invested in them with an intent focus to train and equip them for when He was no longer there. He corrected them when needed and then sent them on their own journey. As a mom, you must equip your children by giving them the tools they need and then, at some point, extend that grace by sending them out. I am not in that season of being a mom, but pray that God grants me the time to get there. We are not promised another moment, day, or month. How are you doing when it comes to extending equipping grace? Spiritual investments will never return void.

Return to page one of this guide, where you wrote down the people who invested in you and modeled how to abide in the Lord. Write them a note this week expressing how thankful you are for them. I guarantee theirs was an intentional act of investment and focus on abiding in Him.

Closing Comments
Withering Roots

I hope you have grown closer than ever to the Lord over these past weeks. I want to conclude our time by looking at our root system. I have never really had what some would call a green thumb. If left in my care, most plants will wither and die. Stephen and I experienced a parenting failure regarding one such plant.

When my son Tyler was in the third grade, he entered an Arbor Day contest at school. He received a postcard that he was to be the recipient of an award because of his entry. I took the postcard, emailed Stephen about the date, and placed it somewhere on my desk's stack of papers. The day came, and we both just forgot about it. The next morning at work, one of the teachers at his elementary school said to Tyler and me, "We missed you at the award ceremony yesterday. Tyler, you got first place. I have your certificate and tree for you."

I stared at her. I then made the connection and realized what had happened. Tyler is our most laid-back child and said, "It's okay, Mom. We can't do everything."

I agreed with him, but it bothered me all week that we missed his moment to accept his award. I have a feeling every time I look at that tree, I am going to be a little bitter. I may even pout a little.

Think about the word "intentional." The definition means "done on purpose, deliberate." Intentional acts of investment develop roots that will sustain those under your influence for days, months, and years to come. As a school counselor, I hear students talk about the constant comparison — that critical sense that someone has more than you. More friends. More likes. More followers. More money.

As followers of Christ, we should have different standards. We are regulated to think differently. As you finish this study, I want you to ask yourselves the following questions:

- What if you thought in terms of the eternal?
- What if you thought about jewels in your crown you have yet to receive?
- What if, in terms of followers, you focused on how you are doing with following Christ instead of who is following you?
- What if you thought of those who will be in heaven one day because of your testimony and investment in others instead of your monetary investments?
- What if you let your guard down and admitted to being flawed instead of pretending to be perfect?

Focus on the word "wither" for a moment. According to Google, the definition is to "become dry, to shrivel up, or to lose vitality, force, or freshness."

I thought about the roots on that tree Tyler won. They must go deep into the ground for that tree to sustain life. A superficial planting will not work.

Spend some time evaluating the roots you are putting down. How deep are they going? Are you teaching your children and grandchildren how to study God's Word? Are you teaching them to pray?

If the only roots you are planting are ones leading to constant comparisons, the spiritual life of the next generation will shrivel. It will be devoid of life and vitality. The only numbers that count are the ones that reap eternal rewards.

Someone will always have more of something. Something will always seem unfair. I am thankful I serve a God of compassion, not one of comparison. A God who sees past my faults and failures and continues to relinquish His mercy and grace on me.

•••••••••••••••••••••

Focus on putting down some intentional roots that will long outlast you.

May God continue to bless you on your journey.

www.ingramcontent.com/pod-product-compliance
Lightning Source LLC
LaVergne TN
LVHW061345060426
835512LV00012B/2568